RUSSIAN HILL — THE S
1853-1906

Volume I of a Neighborhood History

by

William Kostura

Aerie Publications
San Francisco
1997

Published by Aerie Publications
P.O. Box 27365
San Francisco, CA 94127

Previously written by William Kostura:

William F. Lewis: A San Francisco House Builder
        (with Susan Johnson) 1996

Book Design: William Kostura
Page layout/pre-press: Rick Dougherty

ISBN 0-9656400-0-0
Library of Congress Catalog Card Number 96-80350

Russian Hill: The Summit 1853-1906. Volume I of a Neighborhood History.
Author: William Kostura
First edition: 1997

Front cover:

Top: Russian Hill from Nob Hill. Detail from the Eadweard Muybridge panorama of 1878 (Bancroft Library).

Middle row, left to right: Polk-Williams house (California State Library). Edith Livermore and Ethyl Parker, ca. 1900 (courtesy George Livermore). Worcester-Marshall houses, 1030-1036 Vallejo (California State Library).

Bottom row, left to right: Maria Homer and family (courtesy Mrs. Arthur A. Moore). Gelett Burgess (Bancroft Library). Horatio P. Livermore (courtesy George Livermore).

Table of Contents

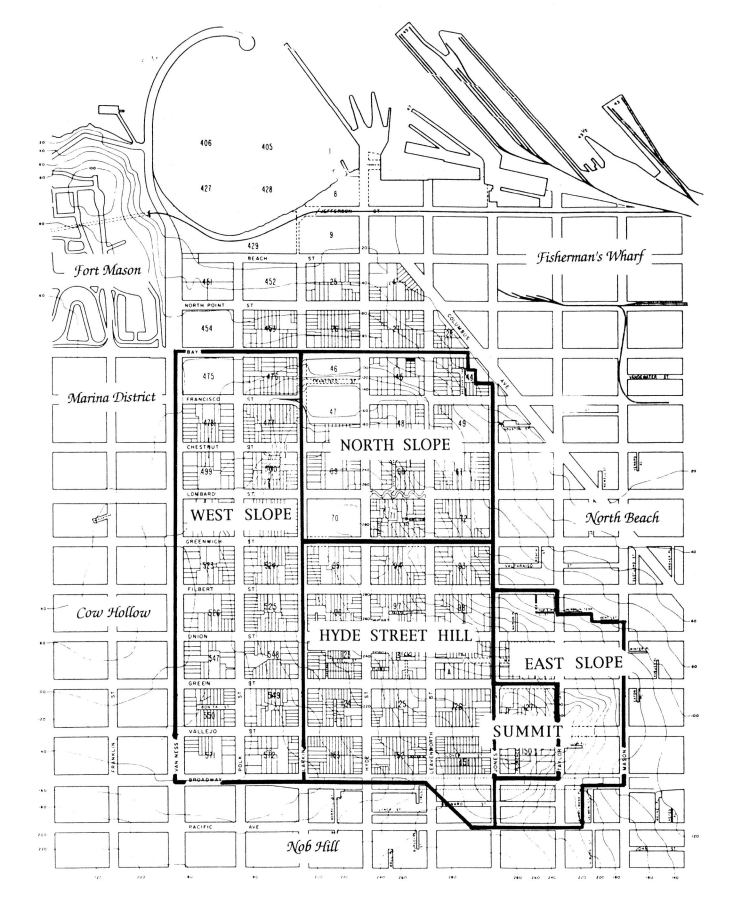

Russian Hill

and Surrounding Neighborhoods
Map courtesy Dept. of City Planning

Author's Note

This book on the history of Russian Hill has evolved in concept a number of times since I began my research in 1981. At that time (I was twenty-eight then), I had no more ambition than to collect such anecdotes as I could find on the subject and to cobble them together into a book. I knew that I would include stories on the Russian graves, Willis Polk, Gelett Burgess, Joseph Worcester, and Frank Demerest on the Summit; and on "Humphreys' Castle," Ina Coolbrith, the octagon house, and the "House of the Flag" on other parts of the hill. Material on such subjects was readily available through a variety of sources, but it had never been gathered together in one place. It seemed to me, then, that gathering such material together was how local history books were usually written. I had no idea then how to do original research, nor how to pull the various stories together into a cohesive narrative history; and I was only faintly aware that I lacked such skills. With a self-confidence based upon blissful ignorance I cheerfully began collecting my anecdotes. Looking back, I can excuse myself, for one has to start somewhere; and I was not far wrong in one thing: that cobbling technique is how local history books have often been written.

Of course, there was no information to be found in books, articles, or library files on the vast majority of the residents and houses of the pre-1906 era. I was convinced, in 1981, that nothing could be done to rectify that situation, for, as everyone said, the city's records had "all burned in 1906." This unfortunate situation was part of the mystique of San Francisco's history.

Fortunately, the mystique was at least half myth. The truth is more interesting. Over the next three years a few knowledgeable historians and researchers directed me to a wealth of resources which make it possible to research virtually every house which has ever stood in San Francisco, and to identify their residents. Real estate and general interest newsletters printed abstracts of deeds beginning in 1865, and architectural journals printed building contracts beginning in the late 1870s. The Spring Valley Water Company tap records survive and date back to 1861. City directories, census records, and indexed newspapers reveal a great deal of information about early San Francisco residents. Most remarkably, many of the official city property records, in the form of the General Index (a complete run from the 1840s to 1906), Deeds (to 1854) and Index to Deeds were available for use in the balcony area of San Francisco's Recorder's Office, at City Hall. (They are now stored in the San Francisco History Archives at the Main Library.) Discovery of these records transformed my ideas of what a Russian Hill history should be.

By adopting a sort of assembly line method, I performed basic research on most houses built on Russian Hill through the 1880s, and many after that date. I traced the ebb and flow of ethnic groups on different parts of the hill. Certain parts of the hill, it became apparent, had possessed distinct characteristics. In order to make the mass of data I had accumulated manageable, I divided Russian Hill into five sub-neighborhoods. These are:

The East Slope. This area was closest to downtown and developed largely during the 1850s. It became a mix of modest rowhouses and larger middle-class residences, and beginning in the 1880s it became more urbanized, as many houses were converted into or replaced by flats. The East Slope acquired its first permanent Italian residents in about 1867. Like the adjacent North Beach neighborhood, it was largely Italian in its makeup by 1906.

The Summit. Members of the building trades established a community here in 1853, and by the 1890s the Summit was notable for its artistic groups and social life. Many of the houses in this area survived the earthquake and fire of 1906, and several of them still stand today.

The North Slope. With its views of the bay and the Golden Gate, this became a neighborhood of elite residences in the 1850s and 1860s. Wealthy and near-wealthy residents lived in fine houses on large, gardened lots. More fine residences were built here at the turn of the century. Part of this neighborhood survived the fire of 1906.

The Hyde Street Hill. This area is impossible to generalize. Russian Hill's largest Victorian mansion was built here in the 1870s, but numerous rowhouses for blue collar workers dotted these blocks as well. A two-block area was solidly Irish during the 1860s-1870s. This part of Russian Hill is best known today for a row of five earthquake and fire survivors on the 1000 block of Green Street, including the Feusier octagon house of 1859.

The West Slope. Located west of Larkin Street, this area developed later than the other parts of Russian Hill. Indeed, its more northern blocks were sparsely settled until well after 1906. The area had much in common with the Marina District to the west.

With detailed research, house by house and resident by resident, patterns of history became clear, and Russian Hill's *genius loci* — its spirit of place — began to emerge. The initial impulses I had felt which led me to choose Russian Hill as the subject of a neighborhood history were greatly strengthened. As I walked the streets of the hill, ghosts dogged my footsteps. In my mind's eye, early residents and vanished buildings came back to life, and they seemed to demand that their stories be told, and that they be rescued from oblivion. A decade later, I no longer feel so strongly obliged to tell each individual's story; it now seems more useful to generalize and search for broader patterns. Still, I cannot completely forget the individual lessons that people and buildings have to tell.

After six or seven years of research I began writing a book. After introductory chapters on the Russian graves and land distribution before the gold rush, I opened with the East Slope, relating its history from 1848 (when the first houses were built) through the early months of 1906. I then turned to the Summit and covered the equivalent period. Like reels of a 1940s serial action movie, or an unfinished story by Scheherazade, my chapter on each sub-neighborhood would end in mid-April, 1906, on the same cliff-hanger note. These chapters would be followed by a chapter on the earthquake and fire, which destroyed most of Russian Hill; by chapters on the rebuilding after the fire; and so forth, up to the high-rise battles of the 1960s. After I had written several hundred pages, I was only one third of the way through my material. I knew the manuscript was becoming unpublishable, that I was telling more than any reader would want to know, and that I would have to reconceptualize this project if it was ever to see print. I put the book aside and turned to other activities, such as publishing short articles, completing a college degree, and developing a career as an historian. Meanwhile, my Russian Hill research sat in file drawers for eight years. I began to wonder if inertia would keep it there forever.

Thanks to the computer revolution, self-publishing has become an option. Here, then, is a volume on the two Summit blocks from 1853 to 1906. I don't know if there is a market for a series of books on one neighborhood, but if there is, I hope to follow with more volumes that will complete the history of Russian Hill through the 1960s. If I may say so without appearing immodest, the story seems to me a great one, full of dramatic events and compelling personalities. I suspect the same is true of most San Francisco neighborhoods, and I strongly believe that each neighborhood should have its written history. San Franciscans identify with their neighborhoods, and such histories should be made available to them.

Still, one might well ask: why spend so much time and energy on a strictly local subject? One way to answer that is to explain that all of my history writing is place oriented. It is about neighborhoods, buildings, and architecture, and about the people who created and lived in the built environment. It is not so much that I am interested in construction techniques or in the finer points of architecture (although I am interested in both of these subjects). It is that buildings in the aggregate, along with the natural topography they are built on, create a certain *feeling* — a sense of place. The variables are infinite, and, unsurprisingly, so are the effects that different combinations have upon us: Victorian buildings vs. those from the 1950s-1960s; flat terrains vs. hills; densely urban neighborhoods vs. single family ones. Telegraph Hill "feels" different from the Sunset district, and San Francisco feels different from Dallas. One is reminded of the Latin term *"genius loci,"* which means "spirit of place." Although the term dates from Roman times, it probably derives from ancient Greece, where all special places had guardian spirits — water sprites, wood dryads, and so forth. The most impressive place, Mt. Olympus, was the home of the gods. I am not saying I believe that great places really have spirits. What I am saying is that we respond to them strongly, as if they do.

We are fast destroying the special qualities of our old neighborhoods. New buildings that are devoid of ornament or surface texture are replacing older houses and flats built with style. Most people like architecture with detailing, fine proportions, careful composition, and colorful and textured materials; and we respond more positively to buildings with these qualities than to those without. It is not just the architecture. When we are aware of their history, we also respond to the events and personages that are associated with older buildings. When the buildings are removed, we lose part of our past.

This book, then, is meant to attune you to any spirits that may still be attached to old places and to serve as a tract for historic preservation. As you walk the streets of Russian Hill... may ghosts follow your footsteps!

On "50-vara lots:"

This book makes occasional reference to the "50-vara lot," once the standard size for land parcels north of Market Street in San Francisco. When land in the downtown area was first surveyed and distributed by Mexican authorities in the 1830s and 1840s, Spanish measurements were naturally used. The vara is a Spanish unit of measurement, thirty-three inches in length, and is roughly equivalent to our yard. The 50-vara lot is a square parcel of land measuring fifty varas (137'6") per side. Each city block north of Market Street is made up of six 50-vara lots, and so measure 100 varas (275') on a north-south axis by 150 varas (412'6") on an east-west axis. During the Mexican period land was assigned to applicants at the rate of one 50-vara lot per resident. After the United States takeover in 1846, the law was amended so that multiple lots could be granted to individuals. Even after 1846, the Spanish unit of measurement continued to be used in land surveys for the sake of consistency. Thus, all of Russian Hill, except for a small area on the West Slope, was surveyed into rectangular blocks of the same size, and all of the land in these blocks was distributed in the form of 50-vara lots. Once a lot was individually owned, of course, its owner could subdivide it into smaller parcels and sell them as he wished. To this day, property north of Market Street and east of Larkin is referred to by title companies and the city as the "50-vara survey."

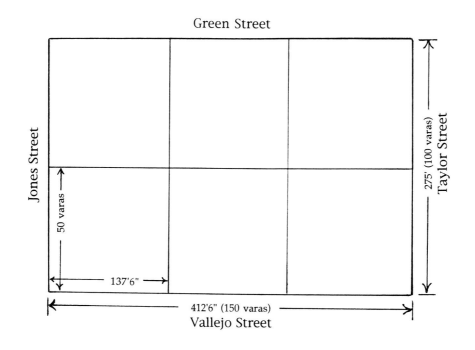

Acknowledgments:

My foremost debt is to George Livermore, the grandson of Horatio Livermore, whom I interviewed on several occasions during the 1980s. I feel fortunate to have visited George at his old family home, 40-42 Florence Street, which still has magnificent redwood paneling as designed by Willis Polk in 1891. George has a remarkably detailed knowledge not only of his own family history, which is central to that of the Summit, but of other personalities and events in his neighborhood. He not only suffered my youthful questioning, but allowed me to borrow family photographs dating to the turn of the century. I also acquired a manuscript chain of title to the William H. Ranlett house (Gillespie and Gray, "Information from an Abstract of Title...") from George. Knowledge gained from him will also be useful in later volumes of this history.

The late Ray Siemers taught me how to use the early city property records — deeds and indexes dating to the gold rush — which were then stored in the Recorder's Office at City Hall. He also taught me how to integrate these records with published deed abstracts in local periodicals and other records. Ray was never able to complete his vast (and rather mysterious) project of sorting out the derivation of San Francisco's early property titles, but I like to think that the techniques he developed will live on through books such as this one.

Rev. Edward G. Capon, the former pastor of the Church of the New Jerusalem, allowed me to spend many hours at the church office studying documents on Joseph Worcester. These letters, memoirs, and other unpublished records greatly enhanced my understanding of Worcester, and I am most grateful.

Richard Muhlberger's article on William H. Ranlett in *Historic Preservation* gave me my first knowledge of Ranlett's east coast career. When I contacted this distinguished art historian, he generously shared with me his unpublished manuscript on Ranlett, which contained much additional information. During his visit to San Francisco at a later date, we visited Ranlett's old haunts on Russian Hill, and he agreed that the Atkinson house was very likely designed by Ranlett.

Mrs. Arthur A. Moore, of Fremont, is the great-granddaughter of Charles and Maria Homer, and graciously allowed me to copy family photographs dating to the 1850s. This fine collection greatly enhanced this book. To Alan H. Nichols I am grateful for permission to copy historic photos of the Atkinson house, and to photograph its Willis Polk-designed interior.

Woody Minor, Alameda historian, read this book in manuscript, performed copy-editing tasks, and offered many valuable suggestions. His perceptive thoughts on the architecture of Joseph Worcester were especially welcome.

Gray Brechin, Joe Butler, Greg Gaar (provider of historic photographs), Gary Goss, Rev. James Lawrence, Neil Malloch, Larry McDonald, Marvin Nathan, and others contributed to this book in important ways. Some of their contributions will bear mention in greater detail in later volumes. My friend Susan Marina Johnson, with whom I have worked on several history projects, has long been aware of my research on Russian Hill. That she found some of my subjects — Ranlett, Demerest, Worcester, Burgess, Polk, the Livermores and others — of interest gave me impetus to continue working over the years.

Map of The Summit, 1853-1893

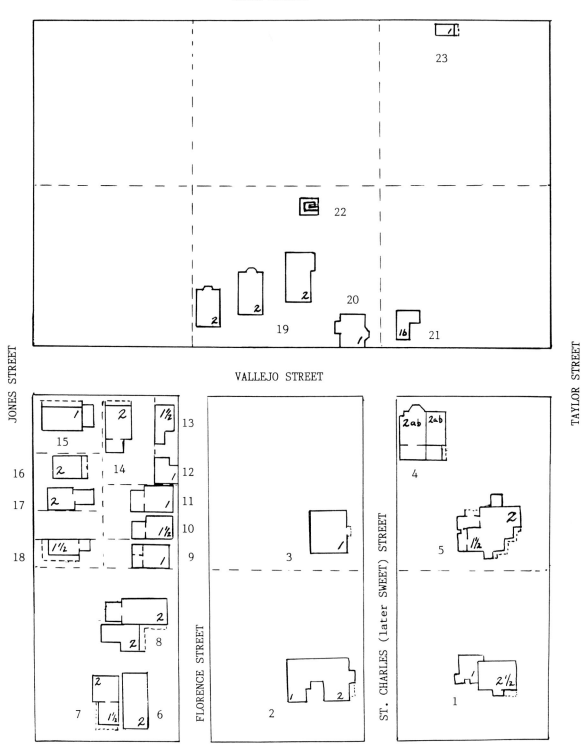

GREEN STREET

VALLEJO STREET

BROADWAY

JONES STREET

TAYLOR STREET

FLORENCE STREET

ST. CHARLES (later SWEET) STREET

Annotations to Map

1. 1601 Taylor
   Built in 1853 by Charles Homer, contractor
   Architect: probably William H. Ranlett
   Demolished in 1910

2. 1032 Broadway (official City Landmark #97)
   Built in 1853 by Joseph H. Atkinson, contractor
   Architect: probably William H. Ranlett
   First floor interior remodeled by architect Willis Polk in 1893 (extant)
   Extant; altered with a coat of stucco 1906-1913, leaving ornament intact

3. 40 Florence (previously 1023 Vallejo, 1045 Vallejo, and 40-42 Florence)
   Built in 1854 by David M. Morrison, contractor
   Subsequent residents include:
       George R. Turner, engineer and surveyor, 1862-1874
       Willis Polk, architect, 1891-1892
       Horatio P. Livermore, industrialist, beginning 1897
   First floor interior remodeled 1891 by Willis Polk; extant
   Additions made 1870s, 1897-1898, 1903, 1987-1988 (Robert A. W. Stern)
   Extant (appearance dates to 1988)

4. 1013-1019 Vallejo
   Built in 1892-1893 by Willis Webb Polk (1013-1017) and Dora Williams (1019)
   Architect: Willis Jefferson Polk
   Extant

5. 1637 Taylor (originally #1607)
   Built in 1853-1854 by William H. Ranlett, architect
   North half removed ca. 1895; remainder altered 1940s-1950s by Jacques Schnier, artist
   Extant (appearance dates mainly to 1950s)

6. 1078 Broadway
   Built in 1863 by James H. Demerest, brick mason
   Burned in 1906

7. 1080 Broadway
   Built in 1853 or 1854 by George D. Nagle, brick contractor
   Subsequent residents:
       Elisha Hall, Jr., carpenter (1858-1861)
       Peter T. Lundberg, newspaper carrier (1861-1890s)
       Geraldo Lyon, steamship cook and steward (1900-1902)
   Burned in 1906

8. 3 Florence and 5 Florence
   Built between 1857-1863 under common ownership
   Residents: John Horgan, pressman (1863); Curtis Williams, master mariner (beg. 1867)
   Burned in 1906

9. 9 Florence
   Built between 1854-1857
   Resident: Gordon Bishop, teamster (1860-1872)
   Burned in 1906

10. 13 Florence
    Built before 1885
    Burned in 1906

11. 15 Florence
    Built in 1855 by William Boyle, blacksmith
    Burned in 1906

12. 17 Florence
    Built ca. 1858 by Henry James Johnson, seaman on steamers *Cortez* and *Columbia*
    Burned in 1906

13. 931 Vallejo (later 1031)
    Built ca. 1866 by Francis O. H. Williams, compositor for the *Evening Bulletin*
    Later resident: Frank Gelett Burgess (1894-1897)
    Burned in 1906

14. 935 Vallejo (later 1035)
    Built between 1857 and 1862
    Subsequent residents:
        Coleman O'Grady, stonemason (1873-1876)
        Peter Lowrey, carpenter (1879-1906)
    Burned in 1906

15. 941 Vallejo (later 1041)
    Built 1853-1854 by Edward Petit
    Subsequent residents:
        James McCarthey, blacksmith (1868)
        Will Irwin, editor (1902-1903)
    Burned in 1906

16. 1718 Jones
    Built between 1854 and 1857
    Burned in 1906

17. 1716 Jones
    Built between 1854 and 1857
    Burned in 1906

18. 1712 Jones
    Built in 1854 by James Egan, laborer
    Burned in 1906

19. 1032-1034-1036 Vallejo
    Built in 1888-1889 by David and Emilie Marshall
    Designed by Rev. Joseph Worcester
    Residents: Thomas and Mary Curtis Richardson (1032; beg. 1889)
    1032 demolished 1960s; 1034 and 1036 are extant

20. 1030 Vallejo
    Built in 1889-1890 for Rev. Joseph Worcester
    Designed by Worcester
    Demolished 1960s

21. Northwest corner of Vallejo and Taylor
    Built in 1853 or 1854
    Residents:
        Samuel Y. Baker, carpenter (1858-1862)
        Margaret Richards, nurse (1862-1873)
        Hall Hanlon, merchant (1862-1865)
        Edward Dillon, chronometer and watch maker (1867-1875)
    Demolished 1875

22. Jobson's Observatory
    Built in ca. 1861 by David Jobson, merchant
    Demolished in ca. 1869

23. Southwest corner of Green and Taylor
    Built before 1856
    Residents:
        Possibly Mary P. Smith (1854)
        Ann Stratman and John Stratman (1856-1861)
        Spencer Blackwell, bookkeeper, packer, clerk (1878-1883)
    Demolished by 1885

Prologue

These two blocks, more than any other portion of Russian Hill, have always been central to the neighborhood's identity. The hill rises to its highest elevation, 360' above sea level, in the more northern of these two blocks, between Vallejo and Green. It was in the southern block that the Russian sailors who gave the hill its name were buried. These graves, located on land now bounded by Broadway, Vallejo, Florence, and Jones streets, were found by the 49ers in the gold rush, and the name "Russian Hill" was given to the site.[1] Although in the 1850s the term was sometimes applied to the entire north-south ridge that today includes Nob and Russian hills, it often had a more specific meaning, namely, the two summit blocks. A conspicuous tower called Jobson's Observatory, in the 1860s; the distinctive architecture of 1853-1854, and later of 1888-1893; and the artists, writers, and architects who congregated there in the 1890s have all helped, at various times, to focus the attention of San Franciscans on the Summit when they thought of Russian Hill. People of all eras have enjoyed climbing to the top of Vallejo Street for the views and for the invigorating effort that is required to attain them.

Hilltops generally, in San Francisco, have been considered to be special places, and their summits have sometimes been reserved for park purposes. Although the summit of Russian Hill has never been a park, these two blocks do have a somewhat park-like setting. This is due in part to the fact that a few of the houses sit on unusually large lots, and that an eighty-five foot lot on Green Street is currently undeveloped. The main reason, however, is that Vallejo and Green streets turn into "streets of steps" between Taylor and Jones. On Green Street the steps pass alongside a considerable expanse of greenery planted in the right-of-way, whereas on Vallejo Street the architectural pathway designed by Willis Polk is more formal. From the curved, balustraded carriage turnaround at mid-block on Vallejo there descends easterly a stairway, also balustraded, which zig-zags through foliage and terminates at Taylor Street, just opposite Coolbrith Park. Finally, two small streets, Florence and Russian Hill Place, branch off of Vallejo Street, and although they are accessible to autos they are really more like pedestrian paths. Everything about the Summit is pedestrian oriented, in fact. To distinguish it further from the surrounding city, tall retaining walls on Broadway and Taylor streets define the boundaries of the summit, setting it apart physically and giving it a fortress-like aspect.

Except, then, for periodic bursts of construction activity (such as in recent years), the Summit has been an island of relative serenity, surrounded by more conventional patterns of urban traffic. As George Livermore recently reminisced, regarding growing up on the Summit in the 1920s, "We lived virtually 'downtown' in a world city, but remained insulated by the quiet of three streets that dead-ended into our quiet world."[2] Mabel H. Collyer wrote for a newspaper in 1912 that "the very steepness, deplored by non-residents only, is an asset which lends the hill intrinsic charm." She contrasted the crowded surrounding neighborhoods to Russian Hill's summit.[3] Earlier still, in 1897, the photographer Arnold Genthe found solace on the Summit as he struggled with a career choice and the decision whether to stay in San Francisco or return to Germany:

> It is a habit of mine, when troubled in thought, to go for a long walk. One late afternoon I found myself at the top of Russian Hill. Around me ran the full circle

"Russian Hill: A Suburb Within a City." Drawn by Willis Polk in 1891,
and published in the *Examiner* on January 28, 1894.

of what I would be giving up if I were to leave San Francisco, a city I had grown to love and where I had made so many fine friendships. I began to see clearly that teaching would never bring me the happiness I wanted. It was here I belonged....[4]

In her 1896 story "A Gracious Visitation" writer Emma Frances Dawson attempted with three passages to evoke the sometimes mystical sensations one gets from being in special places. Her protagonist, Mrs. Trevelyan, lives in the southern block of the Summit, on Florence or Jones:

> I live in a region of remote sounds. On Russian Hill I looked down as from a balloon; all there is of the stir of the city comes in distant bells and whistles, changing their sound, just as the scenery moves, according to the state of the atmosphere. The islands shift as if enchanted, now near and plain, then removed and dim.

> On my way home I went on the green hilltop. All the southern portion of the city was shrouded in smoke... no more of the town in sight than as if the Last Hour had long been burning it. Against the east side of the Swedenborgian minister's hermitage a tall clump of scarlet passion flowers added its solemn legend to the scene.

We left the square, following Powell street, and turned up Vallejo, where Russian Hill seemed to rise to meet and listen to us, dark, sinister even with its lanterns [street lights], like a ladder of light for several almost upright blocks. It took the part of a third person in our talk, the one who knew most.[5]

Geography alone would be enough to create for the Summit a sense of place and to set it apart from its neighbors, but these two blocks have other distinctions. Several important themes run through the Summit's history, and as it happens these themes are symbolized by surviving houses, some dating back to the 1850s. The three builders, Homer, Ranlett, and Atkinson, who founded a community here in 1853-1854; the artists and writers of the 1890s, Gelett Burgess and *Les Jeunes;* the Swedenborgian minister Joseph Worcester and his circle of friends; the Livermore family, which developed so much of the Summit; and the architecture of Willis Polk are all represented by extant structures. As one might expect, these themes overlap — Polk knew the Livermores, Worcester, *Les Jeunes* and an Atkinson, for instance — and several of the buildings symbolize more than one theme. The past, then, seems constantly present here, evoked by early architecture.

A Summit Chronology
1848-1886

September, 1848	William Squire Clark obtains the entire block bounded by Broadway, Vallejo, Taylor and Jones as six 50-vara lots, for $37.50 each.
January, 1853	The partnership of Homer, Ranlett, and Atkinson is formed.
February, 1853	Charles Homer buys the block bounded by Broadway, Vallejo, Taylor and Jones from Clark for $5000. He builds his home at the northwest corner of Broadway and Taylor.
September, 1853	Homer sells the 50-vara lot at the northeast corner of Broadway and Florence to Joseph H. Atkinson for $4000. Atkinson builds the family home, today numbered 1032 Broadway.
	Homer sells the 50-vara lot at the northeast corner of Broadway and Florence to George D. Nagle for $4000. Nagle builds his home here.
October, 1853	Homer sells the 50-vara lot at the southeast corner of Vallejo and Taylor to William H. Ranlett for $4000. Ranlett builds his house, today numbered 1637 Taylor.
May, 1854	Homer sells the 50-vara lot at the southeast corner of Vallejo and Florence to David M. Morrison. Morrison builds his house, now greatly expanded and numbered 40 Florence.
December, 1854	Homer moves to Washington D. C. to attempt to obtain final payment for building the U. S. Marine Hospital. He remains there through 1857.
	Ranlett sells his share of Lone Mountain Cemetery to Joseph H. Atkinson.
ca. 1854	The Stratman house is built at the southeast corner of Green and Taylor. It is torn down in ca. 1884 by Joseph Britton.
	The Baker-Richards house at the northwest corner of Vallejo and Taylor is built. It is torn down in ca. 1875 by Joseph Britton.
ca. 1854-1856	Almarin Brooks Paul and William H. Rhodes move into the Atkinson home, 1032 Broadway, as boarders. Rhodes leaves in 1857.
March 30, 1856	Death of David M. Morrison at the Insane Asylum in Stockton.
ca. 1856-1857	Ranlett abandons his home and returns east to New Jersey.
June 7, 1857	Almarin B. Paul marries Kate V. Mullen, then moves to Nevada City to build a quartz mill. He moves to Nevada in 1859.
1860-1863	Pierre B. and Georgie Cornwall live in the Ranlett house.
1861	Charles Homer departs from San Francisco for the last time, leaving his family on Russian Hill.
	Jobson's Observatory is built on the north block of the Summit. It stands until 1869.
1862-1863	Charles B. Gifford lives on Florence and Jones streets and publishes his five-panel panorama of the city from RH.
1862-1874	George R. and Mary Turner live at the Morrison house.
1863	James H. Demerest builds 1078 Broadway at the northwest corner of Florence.

1863	Charles H. Parker moves into the Homer house as a boarder. He marries Ella Homer in 1871.
	Samuel L. Theller purchases and moves into the Ranlett house. He builds the retaining wall in front of his property when the 1600 block of Taylor is graded in 1866.
1866 or 1867	Almarin B. Paul returns to San Francisco and the Atkinson house.
1874-1879	Peter G. Partridge lives at the Morrison house.
July 28, 1875	Death of June Atkinson.
1877	Taylor Street is graded from Vallejo to Green. Joseph Britton builds a retaining wall along the west side of this block of Taylor Street to preserve his property from erosion.
July 7, 1880	Death of Joseph H. Atkinson.
1886	Samuel L. Theller moves away from the Ranlett house.

Homer-Parker residence, 1601 Taylor Street. Courtesy Mrs. Arthur A. Moore.

Homer, Ranlett and Atkinson

The story effectively begins on February 12, 1853. On that day a building contractor named Charles Homer and his wife, Maria, purchased the entire block bounded by Broadway, Vallejo, Taylor and Jones streets from its first owner, William Squire Clark. The block was empty of buildings then, and was unchanged from its natural state, save for the Russian graveyard (near Jones Street) that had given Russian Hill its name. William Squire Clark had obtained this block from the city government four and one-half years earlier as six 50-vara lots, paying a nominal fee of $37.50 per lot. He held on to the land through the gold rush, while the city expanded and the land appreciated in value. The $5,000 Clark received from Charles and Maria Homer for this block was almost pure profit.[6]

Charles Homer did better with the property, and over a shorter period of time. He had the block re-surveyed so that two streets, Florence and St. Charles, ran through it, providing access to the interior, and over the next two years he sold most of the land for about $20,000, retaining for himself the 50-vara lot at the northwest corner of Broadway and Taylor. Here he built a rather large Gothic revival house for himself and his family.

In a very unusual pattern of sales and development, Homer sold most of his property on this Summit block to people he knew and had worked with. These were people who, like Homer himself, were in the building trades; they built their own homes here, and thus the Summit became a community of people who shared common experiences and business interests. As we shall see, financial difficulties and illness tore this community apart within a few years. Nevertheless, two of the early families remained here for several decades, leaving the hill rich in history and architecture.

Charles Homer was born in

Maria Homer. Courtesy Mrs. Arthur A. Moore.

Massachusetts in 1811 and married Maria Clark Stone there in 1836. They moved at first to central Illinois and then, in the early 1840s, to St. Louis, Missouri. Whether he found success there is unknown, but evidently the lure of the gold rush, and his position close to the departure point for wagon trains, proved too strong for Charles Homer to resist. In 1849 he purchased equipment, joined a company for the journey west, and bid farewell to his wife and their two children.[7]

He underestimated the difficulty of crossing the western half of the continent and had to jettison his belongings on the trail. Nevertheless, he could write to Maria, "Many, many were the times I thought how much you would enjoy the scene before me. How truly wonderful are the works of nature and God. With all the fatigue of the journey I shall never regret taking it."[8] In California he worked the gold fields profitably and then settled in Sacramento, where he also seems to have done well. He purchased a few lots of Sacramento real estate and probably worked as a building contractor in that city. In the spring of 1850 he was the foreman of a construction crew that built a two story, $25,000 commercial building for a merchant named Almarin B. Paul.[9] (Like Homer, Paul was from St. Louis. The two men would later be neighbors on Russian Hill.) By early 1851 Homer seems to have made the decision to settle permanently in California. Maria came to join him, arriving in March on the steamer *Panama*, and the couple moved to San Francisco, where Charles became quite active as a builder.[10]

He built, in fact, what was probably the largest building in San Francisco prior to the construction of Fort Point in the 1860s. This was the U. S. Marine Hospital, a four-story, H-shaped building erected at Rincon Point in 1852-1853. Designed in Washington D. C. by the Treasury Department's architect, Ammi B. Young, construction was supervised locally by architect Reuben Clark.[11] As the primary contractor, Homer must have had the responsibility of selecting all of the sub-contractors, perhaps the most important of which was the brick contractor, that is, the supplier of the hundreds of thousands of bricks

U. S. Marine Hospital, built by Charles Homer in 1853. From *The Annals of San Francisco*.

that would go into erecting this enormous federal project. He chose George D. Nagle, another future neighbor on Russian Hill.

Of Homer's other commissions, only three are known, all two-story brick school houses built for the city government in 1854. These schools are additional evidence of Homer's ability to land important civic commissions. Those on Union Street near Kearny and at the corner of Francisco and Stockton were fine examples of the classical revival and Greek revival styles, while the third, at Bush and Stockton, was more modestly scaled and ornamented.[12]

Whatever else Homer built, it is clear that for some commissions he formed a partnership to facilitate the design and construction of his buildings. The partnership was known as "Homer, Ranlett, and Atkinson" and only lasted for two years, 1853-1854. It may or may not have built much — we simply do not know. But it clearly led to the formation of the community on Russian Hill.[13]

One of Homer's partners was Joseph H. Atkinson, who was born in Pennsylvania in 1816 and moved to Cincinnati, Ohio sometime before 1842. There he worked as a bricklayer and married June S. Mullen, also from Pennsylvania and a year his senior. Their only child, Catherine, was born in 1845. By the time of the gold rush it appears that Atkinson had moved up in the world, becoming a contractor in the brick-laying business, and not merely a laborer in that field.[14]

Atkinson left Cincinnati during the gold rush, choosing against the overland route and instead going to Panama, where he crossed the isthmus and boarded the steamer *Carolina*, arriving in San Francisco in May, 1850.[15] June and Catherine probably followed soon afterward, once Joseph was established in this raw, fast-growing city. The record of his activities during the early 1850s is nearly non-existent, but he appears to have worked

The Atkinson residence, 1032 Broadway.
Courtesy Mrs. Arthur A. Moore.

variously as a brick-laying contractor and a building contractor. Tradition has it that he built the early prison buildings at San Quentin, but of this there is no proof. What is known is that he became part of the Homer, Ranlett, and Atkinson partnership in January, 1853. Then, in September of that year, he purchased a 50-vara lot at the northeast corner of Broadway and Florence from Charles and Maria Homer, for $4,000.[16] On this lot, midway between Taylor and Jones streets, he built a house for himself and his family, becoming next-door neighbors to the Homers. It would be home for the three Atkinsons for the rest of their lives, well into this century. Numbered 1032 Broadway, the house still stands with most of its Italianate detailing intact, and is an official City Landmark. In fact, it was one of the first Italianate villas built in San Francisco, and is the oldest remaining.

The Atkinson residence was almost certainly designed by the third member of the Homer partnership to build on Russian Hill, an architect named William H. Ranlett. Ranlett's own house was also remarkable, and in fact rather startled architectural observers with its several setbacks and corners and its prominent profile on the brow of Russian Hill.

It enjoyed something like local fame into the 1890s. Then, unfortunately, the mutilations that have plagued this house for most of its existence began, and although it still stands, numbered 1637 Taylor, Ranlett himself would not recognize it today. Still, the house has a remarkable history, one even more interesting and bizarre than the architecture that first made it famous.

That history begins with its first owner, who at age forty-three was one of the older participants of the gold rush. A successful New York architect, publisher of a prestigious journal, and a family man with a fine Staten Island home, Ranlett seems like an unlikely person to have embarked upon the hazards of the gold migration. His motive may have been discovered by art historian Richard Muhlberger, who has studied Ranlett's east coast career. According to Muhlberger, the architect's "passion was travel literature, the more exotic, the better." Ranlett may have felt that the California gold rush was his last chance for adventure.[17]

William H. Ranlett was born in Augusta, Maine in 1806. At age thirty-four he moved to New York City, where he joined in partnership with a newly arrived English architect, Joseph C. Wells. The two rented office space on Wall street, and although their partnership lasted only a year, it was enough to establish them; each did well after going his own way.

Ranlett specialized in domestic architecture, designing houses for suburban and rural sites. In his choice of styles he was eclectic, and was obviously influenced by those two exponents of picturesque architecture, Alexander Jackson Davis and Andrew Jackson Downing. These two men, working separately and as friends, had led a major reaction in the 1830s and 1840s against the ubiquitous Greek revival style. Davis designed the first Gothic revival houses in America, while his friend Downing, a landscape architect, published two

William H. Ranlett. From *The Architect*.

widely distributed books, *Cottage Residences* (1842) and *The Architecture of Country Houses* (1850). Downing's books were filled with illustrations of Gothic, Italianate, Romanesque, and simple board-and-batten houses — anything but Greek — set in rustic gardens. By the 1850s Downing and Davis had considerably romanticized the American domestic architectural scene.[18]

Ranlett was an early convert. In 1846 he used the Gothic revival style when he remodeled a pre-Revolutionary War house called the Hermitage, located in Ho-Ho-Kus, New Jersey. (It is now owned by the state and is open to the public.) In 1847 he used the Italianate style for a house in Oswego, New York, which also still stands.[19] But in some ways Ranlett went rather beyond what Downing had done. Beginning in summer, 1846 he issued his own journal, *The Architect*, in a large,

expensively produced format. In it he published elevations and plans of "ornamental cottages and villas" designed by him, including landscape plans, decorative details, specifications, costs, and philosophical essays. The journal had far more lavish production values than Downing's books, and his free-wheeling floor plans were sometimes more imaginative. *The Architect* illustrated a wide range of styles — Gothic, Italianate, Swiss, Tudor, Romanesque, and even "Anglo-Grecian" — and by so doing it not only advertised Ranlett's versatility, it advanced the Romantic picturesque philosophy of dotting the landscape with architectural variety. The periodical found a wide audience; houses based at least in part on designs in *The Architect* have been found in Georgia, Maryland, North Carolina and Mississippi.[20]

Other designs by Ranlett appeared in the prestigious *Godey's Lady's Book*, a contemporary periodical. Ranlett was now fashionable as well as financially successful. He married, to Adelaide Sexton of New Jersey, and the two settled on Staten Island, where as the only architect on the island Ranlett designed many fine homes. His own cottage occupied a large wooded estate with a brook, fruit orchard, and flower garden. He was quite conscious of Staten Island's natural beauty, and thought its hills, fresh air, and views an excellent antidote to the stresses of Manhattan.[21]

In the last issue of *The Architect* Ranlett announced a new journal, *The City Architect*, which would focus on urban architecture. This plan was suddenly abandoned with the news from California of a rich gold strike. Sensing opportunity, seeking adventure, or both, Ranlett reacted quickly. Explaining he would be away for some months, he placed his architectural practice in the hands of an associate and made his way to New Orleans. There, on January 16, 1849, he boarded the bark *Florida* for the voyage around Cape Horn, arriving in California several months later.[22]

Sometime after his arrival, Ranlett's plans must have changed. His temporary stay took on the character of a permanent residence, and he became deeply enmeshed in the economy of San Francisco.

We do not know if he ever went to the gold fields. Certainly he could not live strictly as an architect, for almost no one in the state was interested in architectural niceties during the early years of the gold rush. Building owners were interested in quick profits and generally expected to return east after obtaining them. Houses were prefab affairs shipped around the Horn, and cities were motley collections of impermanent structures which frequently burned. Accordingly, Ranlett had to adapt his skills in imaginative ways to survive. May, 1850 found him operating a storage warehouse and two lumber yards, and he continued to sell lumber into 1852. He found work on at least one occasion, in 1850, as a mapmaker in Sonoma County.[23] Like many others, Ranlett found that there was little use for refined specialists in the business of turning the remote village of San Francisco into a metropolis.

Perhaps the new city's government was as primitive as its architecture; or perhaps, since everyone was a newcomer, the social spirit was insufficiently developed to support that government. At any rate, during a trumped up "crime wave" in 1851, five hundred men, mostly merchants and including Ranlett, formed a Committee of Vigilance which took control of the city.[24] It proved to be selective to the point of a double standard in the crimes it prosecuted, and hung four men after poorly conducted trials.

As San Francisco took on an air of permanence, a demand for architects developed. In 1851 Ranlett received a commission from Thomas O. Larkin to design a two story commercial building at Sansome and Merchant streets. The following year he was chosen by the Secretary of the Treasury to design the U. S. Branch Mint and select a suitable site.[25] Although Ranlett was dropped as architect for this project, and his proposed Market Street location was rejected (the federal government chose instead to economize and remodel a building on Commercial Street), he apparently did design one building used for civic purposes. This was the "Custom House Block," a privately owned commercial building built at Sacramento and Sansome in 1853. Its name was derived from the fact that the office of the Custom House rented the top two floors of this building until its own building on Battery Street was finished. As a result of these commissions, Ranlett listed himself in the 1854 city directory as architect of the "Custom House" and "architect of United States Public Buildings," a slight exaggeration.[26]

Ranlett and Charles Homer became associated in 1851 and worked on several projects together during 1851-1853. By 1852 (as shown in the state census) they and their families were living in the same building or next door to each other. Ranlett, by this time, had been joined in San Francisco by his wife

Charles Homer residence, 1601 Taylor, 1850s.
Courtesey Mrs. Arthur A. Moore.

Adelaide and their daughter Abigail, or "Abba." His California adventure was showing signs of becoming a permanent lifestyle.

In January, 1853 the formal partnership of Homer, Ranlett, and Atkinson was formed, and in their projects over the next two years Homer undoubtedly acted as the general contractor, Atkinson as the brick contractor, and Ranlett as the designer.[27] During this same period the three men also began building their family homes on the Summit of Russian Hill.

Their houses were built not quite simultaneously. Homer bought the block of Broadway/Vallejo/Taylor/Jones in February, 1853, and probably began building then; he sold Atkinson his lot in September; and in October he sold the 50-vara lot at the southwest corner of Vallejo and Taylor to Ranlett for $4000. It appears certain that Ranlett was the architect for all three houses. Homer's Gothic house at 1601 Taylor had features strikingly similar to Ranlett's remodeling of the Hermitage in New Jersey. These included a covered porch and a rectangular bay window, both of which were crowned with castellation; Gothic drip moldings over the windows; and a cut-out bargeboard pattern in the gable nearly identical

to that in the Hermitage. More important, though, is the Atkinson house, not only because it still stands, but because it was better architecture.

The Atkinson house has changed little since it was built in 1853. Most notably, a coat of stucco was applied sometime between 1906 and 1913, and a picture window was installed in the 1970s. The basic design, however, including some of the second floor interior, is still Ranlett's. In style and plan it is an Italianate villa, which was a rarity in 1850s San Francisco. It is important to understand that, although the Italianate style makes use of classical detailing, such as pediments, quoins, columns and colonettes, it was intended by Downing and his followers as a romantic style, in opposition to the Greek revival, which was formal. This was achieved through the use of carved, decorative brackets, bay windows, non-classical proportions, and, especially, an asymmetrical plan. The Atkinson house had all of these elements.

The house has two wings; the main, along a north-south axis, with a central pavilion projecting to the east and a bay window on the south; and a subordinate wing on the west,

The Atkinson house, 1032 Broadway, 1850s. Courtesy Mrs. Arthur A. Moore.

"Italian Villa," by William H. Ranlett. From *The Architect.*

Note the identical roof pitch, the central pavilions, the flanking porches and the paired, arched windows.

which itself has a southward projection, making the house roughly U-shaped. The roofline is low-pitched and cross-gabled, with proportions identical to Ranlett's "Italian Villa" in *The Architect* (Design XXXI). The windows are arched (often paired), with triangular pediments above. Carved brackets supported the eaves and the bay window, and a charming covered porch graced the entry. For San Francisco, 1853, the house was a rare example (Rincon Hill excepted) of fine proportions and detailing.

Alas, it was hardly noticed; Ranlett's own house stole the show. Not only was Ranlett's house more prominently sited, its architecture was considered highly unusual. The house was nearly fifty feet wide, but only a third of the mass extended forward to the front plane of the building. The rest was recessed in a series of setbacks, creating numerous corners and wall surfaces, into each of which a window was placed. In 1857 a reporter for the *Alta* newspaper called it "the freak of Ranlett, the architect, who evidently desired to build a house all windows." *California Architect and Building News* referred to it as "the celebrated house of sixteen corners" in 1891, and as late as 1919 the *Chronicle* columnist Edward Morphy identified Ranlett by name and called his home "the famous 'House of Many Corners.'"[28]

The house was nominally an Italianate, with triangular pediments over the windows, a colonetted entry with fanlight, and a false balcony which wrapped around five sides of the house. With its many corners, however, the house was like no other Italianate in San Francisco, nor like any of Ranlett's designs in *The Architect*. The house was unique.

Upon completion of the Ranlett residence, Russian Hill was crowned with houses of decidedly different appearances, a result quite in accordance with picturesque philosophy. The houses had magnificent views of (but were

William H. Ranlett's "House of Many Corners." Courtesy Mrs. Arthur A. Moore.

comfortably distant from) the emerging metropolis downtown, and this must have reminded Ranlett of the views his Staten Island neighborhood had of Manhattan. The grounds of the Summit houses were bare, however, and the streets were scarred from some preliminary grading. Not until planted trees and gardens matured, and a retaining wall was built on Taylor Street a dozen years later, would the hill attain the beauty that Ranlett must have envisioned from the beginning.

Charles Homer sold land on the Summit to others besides Atkinson and Ranlett, of course. There was George D. Nagle, a builder and brick manufacturer whom Homer had hired to supply bricks for the U. S. Marine Hospital. This native of Germantown, Pennsylvania was later a major contractor in the construction of Fort Point, for which he supplied bricks and labor; and he also performed the brick contracting for the batteries at Fort Mason and Angel Island, the Pioneer Woolen Factory, Grace Church, the Grand Hotel, the Flood mansion on Nob Hill, the Hibernia Bank, and other landmarks.[29] Nagle purchased the 50-vara lot at the northeast corner of Broadway and Jones in September, 1853, and built a small Gothic Revival house there.[30] This house stood until it burnt in 1906.

The Summit of Russian Hill, looking northwest from Broadway and Taylor, between 1854 and 1861. From left to right: the Atkinson house at 1032 Broadway; the one story Morrison house; the Homer house, 1601 Taylor; and the Ranlett house, 1607 (1637) Taylor. Note the scarred streets, formed by preliminary grading, and the temporary wooden steps. Courtesy Mrs. Arthur A. Moore.

Another building contractor, David M. Morrison, purchased the 50-vara lot on the south side of Vallejo Street midway between Taylor and Jones in May, 1854.[31] He may be the Morrison of "Morrison and Roofs" listed frequently in Homer's cash book and ledger; if so, Homer had business dealings with him as he did with others he sold land to. Aside from this, and the fact that he was a contractor, nothing is known of his career.[32] On his spacious lot Morrison built a very modest one story house which measured about thirty feet square. Its roof was slightly pitched, almost flat, with overhanging eaves, and a covered porch

protected the entry, which faced St. Charles Street (to the east). The only decorations were an ornamental balustrade atop the porch and moldings above each window. Ranlett, who had shown in *The Architect* many ways by which modest cottages could be beautified, must have been very disappointed with this house. It still stands, unrecognizably, having been absorbed into an ever-growing residence that is now numbered 40 Florence Street.

Five members of the building trades, then, built their homes on 50-vara lots at the Summit of Russian Hill in 1853-1854. Only at the southeast corner of Vallejo and Jones streets,

David M. Morrison residence, SE corner of Vallejo and Florence streets, 1850s. Courtesy of Mrs. Arthur A. Moore.

where Russian and gold rush graves were still evident, did Homer vary his plan. Here, he subdivided the 50-vara lot into eight smaller lots, on which eleven houses were ultimately built. Blue collar workers, including stone and brick masons, carpenters, dressmakers, steamship stewards, a blacksmith, a compositor, a cook, and laborers lived here over the subsequent decades, along with two ship captains, an engineer, an artist, and a well-known writer.[33] One or two of these houses were demolished at the turn of the century, and the fire of 1906 finished off the rest.

Charles Homer's carefully planned community began to unravel only a few years after it was commenced, and the disintegration must have been painful for everyone to behold. Of the five building trade families on the Summit in 1854, only the Atkinson household was truly intact three years later. The other residents of the Summit did not move away simply because they found better opportunity or more pleasant circumstances elsewhere; instead, financial problems and illness destroyed this seemingly stable neighborhood.

It was the U. S. Marine Hospital, the construction of which should have made his fortune, that appears to have given Charles

Homer his greatest trouble. The original specifications for the hospital had called for hollow brick walls, but supplemental contracts, made later, changed that specification to walls of solid brick. In compensation Homer was to be paid an extra fifty-five dollars per thousand bricks, in addition to the original consideration of $140,000. He was told, however, that payment for the additional brickwork would have to wait until Congress had voted the appropriation. Since Homer had already been delayed for a year — he signed the first contract in November, 1851, and had to wait until December, 1852 for the government to secure its Rincon Point site — he probably felt that he had a substantial investment in the project and had no choice but to proceed. He hired his neighbor-to-be, George D. Nagle, to supply the bricks and to lay them up, with the understanding that Nagle would be paid when Homer was.[34]

Other work in addition to the original contract — grading the site, digging a well, laying drains, etc. — was also required. For this extra work, Homer was paid; but when Nagle submitted his bill in January, 1854, Homer

George D. Nagle in later years. From G. W. Sullivan, *Early Days in California.*

25

Above: Three generations of the Homer-Parker family, mid-1880s. From left to right: Ethel Parker, Maria Homer, Mrs. Charles (Ella Homer) Parker, and Lillian M. Parker. Courtesy Mrs. Arthur A. Moore.

At left: Mrs. Charles (Ella Homer) Parker. Courtesy Mrs. Arthur A. Moore.

demurred, arguing that the appropriation *for the brickwork* had not yet been made by Congress. Nagle sued in 1856, and won his case. Perhaps as a result of bad feeling over the dispute Nagle moved away from Russian Hill at about this time.

Homer's response to Nagle's lawsuit had to be made at long distance, in fact from across the continent. In December, 1854, about a year after the hospital was completed, Charles Homer moved to Washington, D. C. to advance before Congress his claim for the balance of his payment. He was still there in 1857 trying to collect the last $20,000. When he finally returned to San Francisco and his family on Russian Hill it was to stay for only a few years or less. By 1861 he was gone again.[35] Why he left, and where he went, is unknown. (In May, 1876 he transferred ownership of the Russian Hill residence and lot to his wife. Family records indicate he died in 1887. In each case, his place of residence is unrecorded.) His wife, Maria, and their daughter, Ella, continued living at 1601 Taylor for the rest of their lives. They took in a boarder, attorney Charles H. Parker, in 1863, and in 1871, when he was forty-five and she was twenty-six, Parker married Ella Homer. The couple had three children, Homer, Lillian, and Ethel, all three of whom married and also lived in this house.[36] These people seem to have had a very strong family structure, but the man who brought the family west to San Francisco and built their house was no longer with them.

David M. Morrison, the most obscure of the building contractors on Homer's Summit block, enjoyed his hilltop home for less than two years. Although he was still active in San Francisco as late as February 28, 1856, when he filed a lien at City Hall, he was an inmate of the Insane Asylum at Stockton soon afterward. He died there of "acute mania" on March 30th, at age thirty-one, and was buried at Lone Mountain Cemetery in San Francisco.[37] His

house was sold at a probate sale in 1858 to the mortgage holder and was subsequently rented for two years to the family of a Norwegian merchandise broker named Charles Vincent.

William H. Ranlett's residency in the "House of Many Corners" was also very brief, thanks to a grandiose project which ruined him financially. In November, 1853 Ranlett, an undertaker named Nathaniel Gray,[38] and a real estate speculator named Franklin B. Austin purchased a 320 acre tract of land surrounding Lone Mountain for $14,000, and they announced that immense sums would be spent on beautifying the grounds for a cemetery. "Twenty miles" of lanes (this was a shameless exaggeration) were said to have been cut into the cemetery by the spring of 1854, and arrangements were made for construction of a plank road along Bush Street out to its border. Underbrush was cleared, burial lots were surveyed, and the cemetery was fenced. On May 30th, Lone Mountain Cemetery was opened to much singing and prayer, with oratory by Bishop Kip and Col. Edward D. Baker. Everyone agreed that the cemetery, with landscape design by Ranlett, presented a delightful appearance and was a tremendous improvement upon the unsightly city cemetery, Yerba Buena, where the Main Library is today.[39]

Ranlett acted as the superintendent of the cemetery, but not for long, because he could not meet the costs of improvements. The construction of his home (concurrent with the landscaping of the cemetery grounds) was a drain on his resources, and a severe recession in 1854 must have affected his architectural practice. Meanwhile, sales of cemetery lots were not going well. At a well-advertised auction, few lots were sold, and these at low prices. As the compiler of Nathaniel Gray's personal history noted, "The proprietors had their elephant and they had to take care of him."[40]

Ranlett could not do so. In August, 1854

Atkinson-Paul residence, 1032 Broadway, ca. 1893. Courtesy Alan H. Nichols.

he mortgaged his house for $5000, and in December he sold his share of Lone Mountain to his neighbor, Joseph Atkinson.[41] He must have done so at a considerable loss. How he occupied his time over the next two years is unknown, but in 1856 or 1857 the Ranletts abandoned their home to their creditors and returned to the east coast. After seven or eight years in San Francisco, Ranlett's gold rush adventure was over.[42]

Charles Homer, the Ranletts, the Nagles, and David Morrison — all were absent from the Summit only a few years after they had settled there. Only Homer's wife and daughter, and the Atkinson family, remained of the original five families of builders.

As if to symbolize the Atkinson family's stability, their residence at 1032 Broadway remains the most architecturally intact of all the early Summit houses. It almost seems to have been preserved by the stone plaque that was placed above the doorway:

Except the Lord Build the
House They Labor in Vain
JA   That Build It   JSA
Except the Lord Keep the
City the Watchman Waketh in Vain
MDCCCLIII

Fifty-seven years later, after witnessing tremendous changes to the city, Joseph and

June Atkinson's daughter, Kate, still lived in the house, and she commemorated its longevity with a little book entitled *The Home*. It contained photos of the house, some poetry by Gelett Burgess and others, and was dedicated:

In Loving Memory of
J. H. A. and J. S. A.
The Founders of the Home
November, 1853

Unfortunately, little is known about Joseph and June Atkinson's lives beyond the broad outlines. After purchasing Ranlett's share of Lone Mountain Cemetery, Joseph divided his energies between super-intending that business and working as a builder. During two years, 1863-1864, he was listed in city directories as living elsewhere than Russian Hill, temporarily estranged, perhaps, from his family. At about this time he began dealing in real estate in addition to his other work. This activity very likely involved selling off land in the vicinity of Lone Mountain which he had purchased from Ranlett, but which was outside the cemetery boundaries.

In 1868 the proprietors of Lone Mountain Cemetery, Nathaniel Gray, Atkinson, and C. C. Butler, finally gave up the effort to make it profitable and sold the cemetery to a corporation. That corporation changed the name from the appropriately gloomy "Lone Mountain" to the more cheerful, but meaningless, "Laurel Hill Cemetery." Free to take on a new enterprise, Atkinson began a business called the Pacific Patent Agency, with an office at 615 Sacramento Street. This business did not last and by 1869 he had more or less retired, save for selling real estate. In 1875 June died, at age sixty-six. In 1880, after suffering a paralyzing stroke, Joseph joined his wife in death, leaving their thirty-five year old daughter, Kate, as their only descendent.[43]

Kate was far from alone in the house. Other relatives had come to live at 1032 Broadway, including one by marriage who had arrived as a boarder when the house was nearly new. This permanent boarder was Almarin B. Paul, a man whom the Atkinsons met through Charles Homer. He was primarily a mining engineer, but he also worked, as opportunity presented itself, as need dictated, or by personal inclination, as a merchant, banker, inventor, journalist, bookkeeper, and real estate speculator. Kate Atkinson will be discussed later in this book, for she was central to the Summit's social life in another period of its history. Paul, however, belonged to her parents' generation, and his story must be told first.

Atkinson house, second story window enframed by pilasters and pediment. This window was probably designed in 1853 by William H. Ranlett. Photo by author.

Atkinson-Paul Family Tree

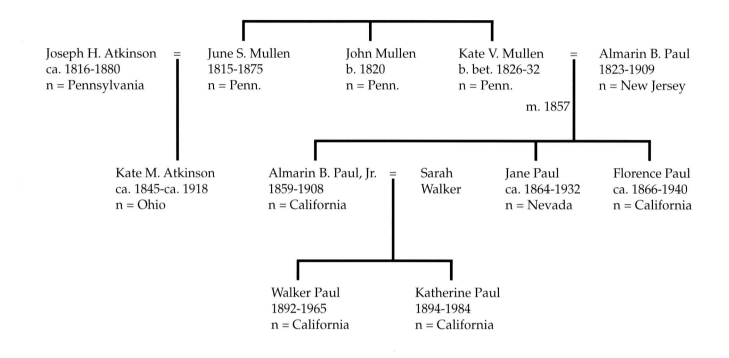

Joseph H. Atkinson
ca. 1816-1880
n = Pennsylvania

=

June S. Mullen
1815-1875
n = Penn.

John Mullen
b. 1820
n = Penn.

Kate V. Mullen
b. bet. 1826-32
n = Penn.

=

Almarin B. Paul
1823-1909
n = New Jersey

m. 1857

Kate M. Atkinson
ca. 1845-ca. 1918
n = Ohio

Almarin B. Paul, Jr.
1859-1908
n = California

=

Sarah
Walker

Jane Paul
ca. 1864-1932
n = Nevada

Florence Paul
ca. 1866-1940
n = California

Walker Paul
1892-1965
n = California

Katherine Paul
1894-1984
n = California

Almarin Brooks Paul

Both Charles Homer and Almarin Paul had lived in St. Louis before the gold rush, and the two men may have known each other there. In the spring of 1850, on J Street in Sacramento, their paths converged again: Almarin Paul was a merchant there, and Charles Homer became the foreman of a construction crew which erected a commercial building for him. Several years later Paul was living in San Francisco, and as a result of his acquaintance with Homer he became a boarder at the Atkinson house on Russian Hill. There he met June Atkinson's sister, Kate V. Mullen, who was eight years his junior. Paul stayed, and in 1857 he married Kate Mullen and became part of the Atkinson family.

Almarin Brooks Paul was born in New Jersey in 1823. In his youth he lived in St. Louis, where he graduated from St. Louis University. He subsequently mined copper and silver in the Lake Superior region and became knowledgeable about the treatment of silver ores. He would find this experience very useful later. Next he returned to St. Louis, where he was working as a dry goods clerk when the gold rush began.[44]

At the first news of gold he went east and twice tried, in late 1848 and early 1849, to sail for California. Failing, he attempted to go overland, but a series of mishaps led to another change in plans. Finally he went to New Orleans whence, with a load of goods, he sailed to Chagres, crossed the isthmus to Panama City, and found passage on the bark *Eugene* to San Francisco, where he arrived on November 3, 1849.

Paul went to Sacramento where he became a wholesale merchant in building hardware and groceries. He did extremely well and invested $25,000 in that two story storefront on J Street that was built by Charles Homer. It was, he said later, "the first well-finished store in Sacramento." However, he soon became restless and left his two partners in this enterprise because he wanted to live in the mountains and do some mining. By early 1851 he was mining gold in Nevada County, and in July of that year he went to New York to try to interest financiers in a quartz mining scheme, to no avail. He returned to Sacramento, where he joined with George Hearst (as Hearst and Co.) in selling merchandise. Alas, the economy had changed there, and this time Paul failed as a merchant. By 1853 he was quite poor, and in possession of a health condition which caused his eyes to fail. With his options running out, he moved to San Francisco.

Despite his near-blindness he did well as a bookkeeper in that city, and he also became a regular correspondent to the St. Louis newspapers. On a better economic footing now, and with his eyesight improved, his entrepreneurial spirit reasserted itself, and in 1854 he went into real estate, specializing in house renting. In this he was also quite successful, making $800-$900 in some months. With Franklin B. Austin, the co-proprietor of Lone Mountain Cemetery, he next attempted to build a road to the Cliff House, but the Board of Supervisors "wanted about half of it [the profits] for passing the bill," he said, so they declined. It was at about this time that Paul, through his association with Charles Homer (or just possibly with Ranlett, through Franklin Austin), moved into the Atkinson house.

When James King of William started the *Bulletin* newspaper in 1855, Paul wrote for it under the penname "Cosmos."[45] When King was shot by James Casey, Paul was at Pioneer Hall an hour later to enroll with other enraged citizens in the revived Vigilance Committee. A few months later he and the former alcalde (mayor), Washington Bartlett, formed their own pro-Vigilance Committee newspaper, the *Daily True Californian*. For an editor, they chose an attorney named William H. Rhodes. Paul and Rhodes must have gotten on quite well, for Rhodes moved into 1032 Broadway with Paul and the Atkinsons.[46]

Paul and Rhodes were an unlikely couple. Paul was a northerner, an entrepreneur, and a miner, while Rhodes was a southerner, an attorney, and far better educated. They both loved writing, however, and both appear to have been a bit hot-headed and unconventional. The current oral tradition that the Atkinson house had been a literary gathering place in its early days undoubtedly derives from these two men.

William H. Rhodes was born in North Carolina in 1822; studied at Princeton and Harvard; and in Galveston, Texas (where his father was U. S. Consul) he opened a law practice. Although he supported the rights of American Indians, which suggests tolerant, humanistic tendencies, and had Irish sympathies, he became a member of the Know Nothing political party, which to a large extent was nativist, anti-foreign, and anti-Catholic (especially anti-Irish). In 1850 he came to San Francisco, practiced law, and wrote for the newspapers.

He and Paul were caught in a bind when the Supreme Court Judge David A. Terry stabbed a Vigilance Committee member nearly to death on the street. Terry was an extremely violent tempered Texan who had worked in Rhodes's law office in Galveston, and Rhodes worked hard to have him released rather than hung by the Vigilance Committee. As a result, although Rhodes and Paul were pro-VC, two other VC papers, the *Daily California Chronicle* (edited by Frank Soule) and the *Alta*, blasted away at Rhodes and the *True Californian*. In its editorials the *True Californian* blasted back. Perhaps as a result, both the *True Californian* and the *Daily California Chronicle* expired in 1857. Paul and Rhodes's newspaper had lasted almost exactly a year, but fortunately neither man depended on this publication for his main income. In Paul's own words, the paper was "more of a love affair than one for profit." In its wake Rhodes left the Atkinson house and Russian Hill. He married in 1859 and formed a household in the Mission district.[47]

On June 5, 1857, two or three months after the failure of the *True Californian*, Almarin B. Paul and Kate V. Mullen were married. Like Rhodes, they left 1032 Broadway then; in fact, they left San Francisco. Paul had resolved to pursue his primary interest — in his own words, "I made up my mind to embrace my loved pursuit mining." Broke again, he borrowed $40 from a friend, went to Nevada City, visited friends who owned a mine, and arranged to build a mill for them for a quarter interest. He now had $18 left, and thus capitalized, he returned to San Francisco, "raised a company, got the money paid in, ordered a mill, and returned to Nevada [City] to erect it. No one suspected I was broke or I never would have been able to raise the mill."

He built the Oriental Quartz Mill in Nevada County, where he and Kate lived for two years. Their stay was interrupted in 1859 by news of the Comstock Lode silver mines in the Nevada Territory. This news electrified Californians, and Paul's old partner George Hearst was one of the very first to head east over the Sierras to explore the possibilities. Hearst managed to buy out one of the Lode's original partners for a paltry $3000 and wrote to Paul strongly advising him to come. Regretfully, Paul sold his share of his quartz mill at a sacrifice so he could do so. His wife Kate returned to her sister's home on Russian Hill in San Francisco, where a son, Almarin B. Paul, Jr., was born. Meanwhile, Almarin went to Virginia City, Nevada, where he could put his knowledge of silver ore reduction, learned at Lake Superior, to good use.

Paul never mined the silver himself. The amount of capital required to do so was

Almarin B. Paul. Courtesy Mrs. Arthur A. Moore.

enormous. What Paul had was important technical knowledge that the mine owners needed. The various mine owners in the Washoe territory were struggling to release the silver from the hard, blue rock in which it was enclosed. Some extremely primitive methods were being used when Paul arrived to organize, with assistance from Hearst, the Washoe Gold and Silver Mining Co. in March, 1860. He sold shares in this ore extraction company, signed contracts with some of the more venturesome mine operators, and then, under a two month deadline, ordered machined-to-order parts at great expense from San Francisco... parts that would have to be hauled by mules over the Sierras. When the machinery arrived, Paul was waiting with completed foundations and cut lumber. Working like a man possessed, Paul assembled a mill of twenty-four huge stamps, settling tanks, amalgamation pans, agitators and separators. He finished on August 11, a day before the deadline, and began extracting silver ore for his clients.[48]

Paul's Pioneer Mills, located near Silver city, several miles south of Virginia City, was a financial success from the beginning, although he quickly had imitators and competitors... very quickly, for another mill of nine stamps commenced operations only a few hours after Paul's. But Paul was first, and he was regarded as the inventor of the "Washoe Process" of reducing ore.

Living conditions were primitive, and soon the awesome din of stamping mills was heard around the clock. Accustomed to the sounds, people awoke in terror once, as if they'd heard some fearsome noise, when a mill ceased stamping ore in the middle of the night. Still, some fine homes and cultural attractions were built, and to this environment Kate Paul came to join her husband. Two daughters were born there: Lulu, who would die four years later in San Francisco, and Jane, who would later become well-known on Russian Hill.

In 1864 Paul tired of his mining enterprises, sold his interests, and became a banker. He opened the banking house of A. B. Paul and Co. with two partners at Gold Hill, but did not do well. As Paul put it in his memoirs years later, "Banking after a year or so I found was not my forte — I was too sympathetic & helped too many 'poor devils' out of trouble. I did not possess that peculiar, cold, selfish, shylock cast for success so I got worsted by this move." Still, Paul had built and sold several mills, owned a great deal of timber and mining acreage, and was reputed to be one of the wealthiest men in Nevada.

One other aspect of Paul's Nevada sojourn must be addressed here.

There has long been an oral tradition that Mark Twain was a visitor to the Atkinson house when he lived in the west.[49] The fact that Paul and Twain were friends in Nevada and met at least once in San Francisco adds a great deal of weight to this story.

They met first in Nevada, when Twain was a staff writer for the *Territorial Enterprise*. One may speculate that their common Missouri background and their mutual love for journalism helped to forge a link between them. At any rate, they worked closely in the spring of 1864 to raise money for the National Sanitary Commission (this was the forerunner of the Red Cross) for the Union troops fighting in the Civil War — Paul as president of the local sanitary fund, Twain through his editorial writing. They reportedly raised pledges of $275,000 in this endeavor, and Paul himself, in his memoir, wrote that he had donated $164,000.[50]

One year earlier, in April, 1863, both Paul and Twain happened to be in San Francisco, and Twain wrote to his sister that "the Hon. A. B. Paul" had introduced him to a young lady in that city.[51] We can only speculate that Paul invited Twain to visit him at 1032 Broadway. Twain was in the city again from June, 1864 to December, 1866, when Paul was generally in

Nevada. Whether he had any reason to visit the Atkinsons in Paul's absence is unknown, but if Paul made any trips to San Francisco during these years, further visits by Twain to the Atkinson house could have occurred then.

The events which led to the Paul family's return to San Francisco, and the Atkinson house, began in about 1866, when Paul sold his bank to the Bank of California. Rich ore was discovered in Inyo County, California, and Paul went to make a careful examination of the country. After doing so, he decided to build a $25,000 mill there. He later wrote:

"This act was the great error of my life — a blot of ten years, and which will ever have my curse of curses. It is proper to state that all told some 300,000$ was expended in these ventures by myself and friends all of which was mainly a dead loss." While there he had begun work on a new process of dry amalgamation. "I quit the country without a dollar, returned to Frisco & commenced further experiments in perfecting the system." His work as an inventor seems to have coincided with Joseph Atkinson's post-Lone Mountain Cemetery career, for in 1867 Atkinson ran the Pacific Patent Agency at 615 Sacramento and Paul had a mining office at the same address. Paul then spent the next ten years (ca. 1867-1877), and $50,000, attempting to simplify and perfect his amalgamation process, for which he obtained several patents. "I lived a life of poverty & having my mind so wholey absorbed," he wrote, "that I thought not of anything else or anybody not even myself & so did a world of injustice to my family — and now that my mind is free of this insanity, as I must term it, I see how great fools inventors can get to be — they surrender all for progress but who cares or appreciates their labors...? Had I my life to live over again I would drive away this mania as a pestilence of ruin to mind, body and death to all family comforts. No scales are large enough to weigh gold enough to pay for my trials —

no success is a compensation. A patent should be good grounds for any woman to procure a divorce upon...."[52]

Sad, if sketchy, corroboration can be found in other sources. In disputing Paul's low estimate of the value of real estate sales during 1870, the *Real Estate Circular* needled, "Almarin B. Paul, who has mining on the brain, and who is noted for looking at only one side of anything he attempts to discuss...."[53] And, while Paul did not quite admit it in his memoir, he appears to have been somewhat estranged from his family for three years. City directories show that he lived at 10 Bernard Street from 1872-1875. This address was only a block away from the Atkinson house, and Paul probably lived there alone, although within easy visiting range of his family. He was probably thinking mainly of these three years when he wrote in his memoir "From 1868 to date I made my residence in San Francisco living quite humble and secluded. Necessity kept my mind active." The year 1876, however, found him back at 1032 Broadway, this time permanently. He never moved away again.

It was a large household, even after the death of June Atkinson in 1875. At the end of 1876 the following people lived at the Atkinson house:

> Joseph H. Atkinson, about 60 (four
>   years before his death)
> Almarin B. Paul, 53
> Kate V. (Mullen) Paul, about 47
> John Mullen (Kate Paul's brother),
>   about 56
> Kate Atkinson (daughter of Joseph
>   and June), age 31
> Almarin B. Paul, Jr., 17
> Jane Paul, 12
> Florence Paul, 10

Additionally, the family always had a servant or two, and in 1880 there was one, Ah

Hang, from China.[54]

During most of the 1870s Paul maintained offices downtown as a mining engineer, tirelessly promoting his inventions. He issued 10,000 pamphlets explaining his system of dry amalgamation in hopes of selling his patents. He set up companies of which he was the director, secretary, etc. He "gained but little [yet] saw plenty of chances of dishonourable gain." In 1878, weary of failure, he ceased his efforts for awhile, but he was back at it again in 1882, when he "made quite an improvement in my arrasta." The penultimate passage in his memoir is hopeful:

"In 1883 I struck on a new idea of amalgamation and which I regard as the great step of my life as it brought forth a cheap mode of perfectly extracting gold, certain classes of silver...," etc. "Ages hence will do me justice though the people around me... honoureth me not. They cannot appreciate advancement, but can a fool if he has gold in his coffers."

The end of his memoir is calmer and more reasoned. "13 Sept. 1883 found me 60 years of age and possessed of good health, wife and 3 grown children. My worldly effects were about balanced by what I owed & hence for old age there was rather a slim show."[55]

Whether Almarin Paul ever realized great profits from his amalgamation experiments is unknown. Long after writing this memoir he continued to maintain an office at various locations downtown, and for a time his son joined him at the office. In his old age, as gold rush argonauts dwindled in numbers, he enjoyed a sort of "grand old man" status, and he rewrote his memoirs of the gold rush years in the form of published articles. These articles are as lively and well written an account of that period as one is likely to find.

Florence Paul, with neighborhood children, at 1032 Broadway, 1880s. Ethel Parker is sitting at lower left. Courtesy Mrs. Arthur A. Moore.

Other Residents of the Summit
1850s-1880s

While Almarin B. Paul came and went from Russian Hill, and struggled with his obsession, other men of large affairs and prominent rank made the Summit their home, with their families. The former Ranlett residence, at the southwest corner of Vallejo and Taylor, attracted the wealthiest of the Summit's residents. In 1860 Pierre B. Cornwall became the first owner-resident of the house after Ranlett was foreclosed upon. Cornwall's great wealth was founded upon a stroke of luck: he came to California in 1848, before news of gold reached the United States, and so was able to buy real estate at fabulously low prices.

Cornwall was born in New York state in 1821 and left for California with hopes of somehow being able to pay off some debts. On the way he was captured by Pawnees and rescued by Sioux, and he then led a wagon train over the Carson Pass, arriving in California in August, 1848. He tried mining only briefly, set up mercantile businesses at the mines and in Sacramento, helped start a bank, and bought lots of real estate. In 1850 he sold his banking interest and two-thirds of his real estate for $640,000. He had made a fortune in only eighteen months.

In the late 1850s Cornwall and his bride, the former Georgia Cutler of Sacramento, moved to San Francisco, where Cornwall set up a real estate and notary public office. During their three years residence in the "House of Many Corners" Cornwall worked as a stockbroker, purchased stock in silver mines, and became one of the forty charter members of the San Francisco Stock and Exchange Board, which was created to trade in such stock. Georgia, however, became very ill at this time, and the Cornwall's sold their house to Samuel L. Theller in October, 1863. She died the following year.[56]

Samuel Theller had come to California in the gold rush; worked at the Isthmus of Panama in the transport business, where he met Cornelius Garrison and William Ralston; then returned to San Francisco where (perhaps through Garrison) he became an associate of F. L. A. Pioche. Pioche and his partners had purchased the vast San Miguel Rancho of Jose de Jesus Noe in 1860, and it was Theller's job to carve up as much of this rancho as possible for sale to "homestead associations" and individuals. Much of Eureka Valley, Noe Valley and other neighborhoods were turned into residential neighborhoods in this way. Later, the owners of the rancho were found to have defrauded the homestead association proprietors by artificially inflating the value of this property, and in this process Theller must have had a hand. Worth several hundred thousand dollars, Theller and his family stayed at the Ranlett house, then numbered 1607 Taylor, for twenty-two years. They sold it in January, 1886.[57]

In 1866 Theller built the handsome stone retaining wall which still exists in front of this house.[58] Its construction became necessary to prevent erosion of his front yard when, in a major street grading operation, 9383 cubic yards of earth were removed from the street right-of-way on the 1600 block of Taylor. Despite this civic improvement Taylor street was still very steep, and it seems doubtful that a horse could draw any kind of a load up the hill, save with extreme difficulty. At the top, where Taylor intersected Vallejo Street, the graded street ended at a man-made cliff. The next block of Taylor to the north was not graded until eleven years later.

*   *   *

The residence of the late David M. Morrison, at the southeast corner of Vallejo and Florence, became the property of real estate dealer Peter G. Partridge in 1862, and was promptly sold by him to George Runcy Turner. Turner was a civil engineer from Massachusetts, and had just finished serving (1857-1861) a term as the city and county surveyor. During the subsequent twelve years Turner worked in various partnerships as a surveyor and engineer, with offices at Parrott's Granite Block and the Merchants' Exchange. In 1863 he married, to Mary Chase White of New Hampshire, and the couple had four children while living at Vallejo and Florence. To their modest cottage the couple made some small improvements, including a bay window on the south side and an orchard on the grounds. This orchard survived for many decades and was considered a striking feature by visitors to the hilltop. In late 1874, however, the Turners defaulted on their house payments, and the county sheriff deeded the house back to Peter G. Partridge, who moved in with his family and remained for five years. Partridge continued dealing in real estate, but he, too, went bankrupt during a local, but major, real estate slump, and he lost this house to a creditor in 1879.[59]

By then the house had been raised up to the second story level and a new first story built underneath it. This had been done either during 1870-1874 by the Turners to accommodate their growing family (perhaps contributing to their default in payments) or during 1875-1877 by the Partridges. The enlarged, far more attractive house can be seen in the Muybridge panoramas of 1877 and 1878 and in later photos. It has its original gently sloped roofline and covered porch, although the latter has now become a second story balcony. The bay window added earlier by Turner now sits above a first story window which is flush with the wall. (A later owner would add a projecting first story bay

The Morrison-Turner-Partridge residence (now 40 Florence) after being raised to become two stories. Courtesy Mrs. Arthur A. Moore.

here as well, one which lined up with the bay window above.)

Also visible in the Muybridge panorama are the many trees planted on the lot by Turner. Both the Homer-Parker and the Samuel Theller lots are also attractively landscaped, while the Atkinson-Paul lot is mostly open lawn. Contrast these four lots with the urban density all around them in the Muybridge photo. With mature plantings, this part of the Summit at last resembled the rustic, picturesque haven from urban ills (but not from economic difficulties) which Ranlett must have envisioned over two decades earlier.

*　　　*　　　*

Thus far we have largely neglected discussion of the smaller houses, and their occupants, located in the blocks between Florence and Jones streets and between Vallejo and Green. In the parlance of the time, the residents of these blocks were not "prominent" in the "affairs of the city," but some of them were stable residents of the Summit whose presence spanned decades.

George D. Nagle's 50-vara lot was subdivided in the 1850s and in 1858 his Gothic cottage was purchased by a carpenter from

Russian Hill from Nob Hill, 1869. Photo by Eadweard Muybridge. At right is the Atkinson house. Directly behind it is the one story Morrison-Turner house. To their left, across Florence Street, one can see the two story Demerest house, the smaller Nagle house (both facing the viewer), and other small houses facing Florence and Jones. At far left one can see the rear of three houses on the 1000 block of Green, all of which still stand. Greg Gaar Collection.

Ohio, Elisha Hall, Jr. Hall stayed only three years, but his successor stayed over thirty. Hall sold the house in 1861 to Peter T. Lundberg, a Swede who carried the *Daily Alta* newspaper. Lundberg and his wife raised a family of eight and lived in this house until the late 1890s. No details are known of their lives, but surely it is a testament to their careful lifestyle that a newspaper carrier could purchase a house built by one of the city's major brick contractors, and support such a large family.

In 1863 a brick mason named James H. Demerest purchased a fifty foot portion of the Nagle lot and built a gabled two-story house at 1078 Broadway, next door to the Lundbergs. Demerest had come to California in 1849, sailing around the horn from Providence, Rhode Island, and went to El Dorado County seeking gold. His wife Phoebe crossed the plains two years later and joined her husband at the mining camp, where their son Frank was born in 1852. The family then moved to San Francisco and lived by the Fort Point construction site where James worked for George Nagle as a mason. The Demerests next boarded at two residences on Russian Hill (on Green near Larkin in 1860, and at 815 Union in 1861-1863) before building their own home at 1078 Broadway. Demerest continued working mostly as a mason over the succeeding decades, punctuating this career with stints as the city jail keeper in 1865 and as a bookkeeper in 1880. He died at age eighty in 1899, and Phoebe lived until 1905. Their son Frank grew to adulthood and lived with them on the Summit most of the time, although not continuously, and he rebuilt on the site after the house burned in 1906. A few people still remember Frank

Looking south from the Summit, 1862. Drawing by Charles B. Gifford. Jobson's Observatory dominates the view. Houses on the west side of Florence Street and the south side of Vallejo are clearly visible, while the flat-roofed Morrison-Turner house is partly obscured by its lattice fence. One of the houses on Florence was Gifford's residence at this time. Greg Gaar Collection.

Demerest and his eccentric, somewhat hermit-like, and occasionally outrageous lifestyle. His story will be continued later in this book and in a succeeding volume.[60]

The peripatetic landscape artist Charles B. Gifford lived just north of the Lundberg and Demerest families in two different houses, on the west side of Florence Street in 1862 and on the east side of Jones in 1863. He was born in Massachusetts in 1830 and lived here with his Nicaragua-born wife Josepha and their two children. During their brief residency on the Summit Gifford made a mark which endures to the present. He is known for his minutely accurate drawings of San Francisco scenes during the 1860s, and these are occasionally reprinted in books and hung in libraries. Hayes Valley, the northern waterfront, Cow Hollow,

and the Mission district were all recorded by this artist, and in 1868 he teamed with William V. Gray to produce a "Bird's Eye View of the City and County of San Francisco," the finest aerial view of the city ever produced. It was published by A. L. Bancroft in 1873.

While living on Florence Street in 1862 Gifford walked across Vallejo Street to the precise summit of the hill and set up his easel, where he drew the largest landscape of his career. This was a five panel, 360 degree panorama of the hill which, in its accuracy and clarity, matches any photographs that have survived to the present. Actually it is better, for none of the photographs have as wide a frame as any of Gifford's panels. This valuable document was published in 1862 and was reprinted the following year.

Looking south along Florence Street, from Vallejo. Here one can see most of the houses on the west side of Florence. The Francis O. H. Williams residence (later Gelett Burgess') is directly behind the gas streetlight. Gelett Burgess Collection, Bancroft Library.

On the south side of Vallejo Street, between Florence and Jones, was a two story house with a front porch which had been built around 1860. A stonemason named Coleman O'Grady came to live there in the mid-1870s, and the house was purchased by a carpenter named Peter Lowrey in 1879. The aged Lowrey was still there when the house burned in 1906, and with the help of his sons he rebuilt on the site soon afterward. Their house, now numbered 1075-1077 Vallejo, still stands today.

Next door, at the southwest corner of Vallejo and Florence streets, a plain, one-story house with a gabled attic was built in about 1866 and was first occupied by Francis O. H. Williams, a compositor for the *Evening Bulletin.* Later, when Gelett Burgess rented here, the place was known as the "Neighborhood House." Other one story houses on Florence were occupied by Curtis Williams, a master mariner; Gordon Bishop, a teamster; and lumberman Enos Merritt; each during the 1860s-1870s.

The more northern block on the Summit remained virtually undeveloped before 1888. Certainly the steep site contributed to this, but the lack of development must still be considered something of a mystery. A very small gabled house at the southwest corner of Green and Taylor was built in ca. 1854 and torn down in about 1884. None of its several known residents stayed for more than five years. (We shall call this the Stratman house, after early residents Ann Stratman, a widow, and John Stratman, a news agent and owner of a downtown circulating library). On the adjacent 50-vara lot, just over the brow of the hill at the northwest corner of Vallejo and Taylor, was another one story house, also built in about 1854. Its first known owner (in 1858) was a carpenter named Samuel Y. Baker. A nurse named Margaret Richards bought the house and lot in ca. 1862, and she lived here for twelve years, first with merchant Hall Hanlon, and then with chronometer and watch maker Edward Dillon, whose office was in the Merchants' Exchange Building. Could Richards and her boarders have been rare nineteenth century practitioners of romantic cohabitation without benefit of legal ceremony? We will probably never know. The Richards house was demolished in about 1875. It and the Stratman house are the only two houses known to have been built on this block before 1888.[61]

The steep heights which made this block difficult of access and unattractive to builders made it useful to one man, a merchant named David Jobson. Like all wholesale and commission merchants, Jobson was vitally interested in learning which ships were arriving with what cargoes at the port of San Francisco, for such arrivals could dramatically affect the prices of commodities. The Merchants' Exchange had long had a system of telegraph stations and telescopes at Land's End and on Telegraph Hill, and, spying ships before they arrived, the Merchants' Exchange sold this

Jobson's Observatory, 1860s. Courtesy Adah Bakalinsky.

intelligence to its subscribers. Any merchant willing to undergo the expense could have set up an alternate infrastructure, but only David Jobson did so. Buying or renting a lot on the very summit of Russian Hill (one lot west of Margaret Richards' house), Jobson erected an observation tower about fifty feet high in 1861. This wood truss girder structure was enclosed on the first level, open above, and surrounded on the outside by a spiral staircase which led to an observation platform at the top. From here, Jobson or his employee could spy incoming ships with a telescope and then rush downtown to buy or sell merchandise accordingly, hopefully in advance of those who got their information from the Merchants' Exchange.

There was a small caretaker's cabin at the base of the tower, and a fence which, according to columnist Edward Morphy (writing fifty years later) enclosed a potato patch and a cow. On Sundays Jobson allowed the public to ascend the tower to enjoy the views, at a cost of two bits for adults and half that for children. During September the Mexican residents of North Beach liked to celebrate their independence day by flying a Mexican flag from the top of the tower and firing cannon

salutes from its base into the city below. In 1868 or 1869, weakened by winds, Jobson's Observatory was considered dangerous and pulled down.[62]

In 1876, when the block bounded by Vallejo, Green, Taylor and Jones streets was once again bare of structures (save for the Stratman house at the corner of Green and Taylor) the block served as a *de facto* park. At least one person thought it should be purchased by the city and made so officially, before more construction occurred. After all, wrote the pseudonymous "Excelsior," the summit of Telegraph Hill had just been purchased for a park, and Russian Hill was higher yet, with "the only very fine view of the Golden Gate to be obtained from any point in the city." The writer had visited the spot frequently during his two years in the city, and "invariably" found several others there as well. "If properly improved it will soon become a very popular place of resort." His plea, however, went unheeded.[63]

One reason may be that in 1876 the block was incredibly difficult of access, at least from the east. Matters weren't really helped the following year when Taylor Street between Vallejo and Green was graded, leaving the land to the west "stranded" high above the new, lower, street level. Soon afterward the owner of the two lots facing Taylor, Joseph Britton, built a high stone retaining wall along Taylor Street.[64] This wall faces Coolbrith Park and in large part still exists. The grading and construction of the retaining wall left a cliff face along Taylor Street, while Vallejo Street (going west from Taylor toward Jones) became a steep zig-zag trail which ultimately became known as the "goat path." Many people traveling from downtown or North Beach chose to attain the Summit by going the long way around, i. e., along Pacific Street to Jones, up Jones to Vallejo, and thence east along Vallejo, avoiding the goat path.

Russian Hill from Telegraph Hill, 1865. Jobson's Observatory and the Margaret Richards house (to its left) are visible on the horizon. To their right, and lower, is the Stratman house. Houses on the south block of the Summit are somewhat obscured. San Francisco History Archives.

In the mid-1880s Joseph Britton demolished the Stratman house and began quarrying the two 50-vara lots facing Taylor, bringing them closer to the street level but breaking up the curve of the hillside. He very likely had development plans for this property, but for some reason he never carried through with them, and so the land remained undeveloped during Britton's lifetime.[65] (One of the lots was finally built upon in 1906, while the other remained vacant until the 1950s.)

With the Stratman and Richards houses gone, the entire block bounded by Vallejo, Green, Taylor and Jones streets was vacant for the next five years, from 1884 until late 1888. Meanwhile, a pattern of development had long been occurring in San Francisco's outer neighborhoods — a pattern which completely bypassed the summit of Russian Hill. Aided by many miles of horsecar and cable car lines, hundreds of blocks of mostly flat land in the Western Addition and the Mission district were being developed with Italianate, Eastlake and Queen Anne rowhouses for middle class San Franciscans. Why build on Russian Hill's steepest slope when so much level real estate was available close to mass transit? Not until 1888-1889 was the Summit's northern block built upon again. Then, four modest houses were built which not only defied prevailing development patterns, but broke completely with Victorian architectural styles. These shingled houses commenced a revolution in San Francisco's domestic architecture. They were designed, not by a prominent architect with social connections or training in the eastern states, but by the pastor of a small and little-known congregation, the Church of the New Jerusalem. When Rev. Joseph Worcester came to Russian Hill, he also began a new era in the Summit's history.

A Summit Chronology
1870, 1888-1898

January, 1870	David P. Marshall buys Jobson Observatory Site on Vallejo Street
October, 1888	Construction begins on three houses on the above lot (1032-1034-1036 Vallejo), to designs by Joseph Worcester
ca. January, 1889	Construction completed on above houses. Thomas and Mary Curtis Richardson move into 1032 Vallejo later this year.
ca. October, 1889	Construction begins on Joseph Worcester's residence, 1030 Vallejo.
December, 1889	Horatio P. Livermore buys the Morrison-Turner-Partridge house, 1023 Vallejo (now 40 Florence).
Jan. or Feb., 1891	Willis Polk's most likely date of occupation of 1023 Vallejo.
September, 1891	Frank Gelett Burgess begins frequent visits to Russian Hill.
1892-1893	Polk-Williams house, 1013-1019 Vallejo, is built.
July-Dec., 1893	Willis Polk remodels the interior of Kate Atkinson's house, 1032 Broadway.
August, 1894	Construction begins on the Swedenborgian Church in Pacific Heights.
Early-mid-1894	Gelett Burgess moves to 1031 Vallejo. The Russian Hill Neighborhood House is organized there in June.
May, 1895	Fanny Stevenson moves in with Dora Williams at 1019 Vallejo.
	The first issue of *The Lark* is published by Burgess and Bruce Porter.
April, 1897	*The Lark* ceases publication.
May, 1897	*The Epi-Lark* is published. Gelett Burgess moves east.
Late 1897-early 1898	The H. P. Livermore family moves into 1023 Vallejo. Shingled additions are made to the house.

Five Panoramas of the Summit

Looking north from Washington and Mason streets, ca. 1865. Jobson's Observatory and the Margaret Richards house are clearly visible on the Summit horizon, as are the Morrison-Turner, Ranlett-Theller, Atkinson, and Homer houses below them. The tall, square house at the SE corner of Vallejo and Taylor, whose flat roof just breaks the horizon, is the House of the Flag, 1652-1656 Taylor, extant today with a shingled addition. Greg Gaar Collection.

Russian Hill from Nob Hill, 1878. Photo by Eadweard Muybridge. This is a detail from the famous Muybridge panorama. From left to right: the Nagle house, the Demerest house, several houses on Florence Street, the Atkinson house, the Morrison-Turner-Partridge house (now grown to two stories), the Homer house (obscured by trees), and the Ranlett-Theller house. Note the stone retaining walls on Taylor Street, necessitated by street grading. Bancroft Library.

Looking northwest from Broadway and Taylor, 1870s. In the center is the Homer residence. At right is the Ranlett-Theller house, and at left, the Morrison-Turner-Partridge house. This is the best view of Ranlett's "House of Many Corners" before it was cut in half. Courtesy Mrs. Arthur A. Moore.

Looking northwest from Broadway and Taylor, between 1898-1903. The Morrison house at upper left has been expanded and shingled by Horatio Livermore, Ranlett's "House of Many Corners" (at right) has been cut in half, and a new retaining wall has just been built on Broadway. The new Willis Polk residence is just visible, above the Ranlett house. Courtesy Mrs. Arthur A. Moore.

The Summit, looking north from Broadway, between 1898-1903. From left to right: the Livermore house, the Polk-Williams house, the Atkinson house, and the Homer house. Note the fine wood balustrade, designed by Willis Polk, that surmounts the new concrete retaining wall. Courtesy Mrs. Arthur A. Moore.

Rev. Joseph Worcester

In 1870 a man named David P. Marshall purchased the 50-vara lot on Vallejo Street where Jobson's Observatory had so recently stood.[66] Marshall did not live on Russian Hill, he would never live on Russian Hill, and he allowed the land to remain vacant for almost nineteen years. No one could have guessed that this idle investment would link Marshall's name with great events in Russian Hill history.

Marshall had been an inspector for the San Francisco Gas Company since 1861. According to historian Richard Dillon, his job took him into virtually every building in San Francisco to inspect gas pipes and tubing. He also supervised the inspection of the city's street lamps and manipulated the valves to the company's two huge gas tanks at Fifth and Howard streets. A Quaker (who had nevertheless fought in the Mexican War), Marshall wore a long linen duster and used a shepherd's crook for a cane. He continued working for the gas company when it merged with another utility to become the San Francisco Gas Light Company, and lived with his wife, Emilie, on the company premises in a small brick house adjacent to the valve house, between the two gas tanks. He lived thus until his death in 1894.[67]

David Marshall had done nothing remarkable with his Russian Hill land... but Emilie Price Marshall did. No Quaker, she was one of twenty-nine founding members of a Swedenborgian congregation called the New Jerusalem Church, which was formed in 1866.[68] It was Emilie who in 1888 asked her pastor, Joseph Worcester, to make use of his talents as an amateur architect and design three houses for her husband's lot on Russian Hill. In 1889 Worcester built his own cottage on the Marshalls' land, next to the group of three, and lived there for over two decades. Here he entertained guests and dispensed advice to

Joseph Worcester. *Examiner,* September 30, 1895.

professional architects and artists who had traveled widely and studied under masters. Although Worcester never had formal training as an architect, nor served an apprenticeship in the field; although he was not an artist, nor a writer, except of letters and sermons; although none of his sermons was ever published, and most were burnt at his death; although his congregation was small, and its members were not prominent; although Worcester did not aspire to social position or business connections; and although he was reticent and self-effacing in his manner; he nevertheless became one of the most admired men in San Francisco, had a strong effect on its architecture, gave advice on artistic matters freely, and profoundly changed the lives of many.

Joseph Worcestor was born in Boston in 1836 into a family of Swedenborgian ministers. His father, grandfather, two brothers, and a nephew all preached to Swedenborgian congregations, and the two brothers, John and Benjamin, both wrote many volumes on this religion.[69] The father strongly hoped that Joseph would also become the pastor of a Massachusetts congregation, but the son had some independent ideas. For one thing, he was not at first certain that he wanted to become a pastor in Massachusetts, or anywhere else. In his youth he studied art and architecture, taught drawing as a young man, and considered architecture as a career. His ideas were influenced by his reading — Emerson, Ruskin, Lowell, and Wordsworth — and by his religious training. He viewed the natural world as a manifestation of God, and felt that buildings should relate well to the environment rather than disrupt it. Nature was beautiful, and buildings which resemble nature were the most beautiful of buildings.

In the end, Worcester continued in the family tradition, continuing his religious training and becoming ordained in 1867. Still he rebelled. Four years before his ordination he made a trip to California, and in San Francisco he conducted some services for the New Church (Swedenborgian) congregation there. He returned to Massachusetts, but that California trip would prove decisive. In 1866 a minority faction arose within the San Francisco congregation, and this group began worshipping apart from the main one. They invited several ministers, unsuccessfully, and in the fall of 1867 they asked Worcester to return to San Francisco to lead them. By one account they had wanted him from the time of his 1863 visit. Soon after his ordination Worcester once again left his home town of Waltham, Massachusetts for California, quite in defiance of his father's wishes.[70]

Joseph's nephew, Alfred Worcester, would write many years later that California had made as strong an impression on Joseph Worcester as he had made upon the San Francisco Swedenborgians. "Having breathed the freer air of California he would have suffocated in a more conservative atmosphere," wrote Alfred. "And devout believer as he was

in Swedenborg's doctrine he yet never could feel at home in the New Church organization. 'It irked him to be here [in Waltham].'"[71] Another influence may have been John Muir, who, according to James Lawrence, the current pastor of the church, met Worcester in the 1860s.[72] Lacking Worcester's own thoughts on the subject, we can only suppose that Muir's vision of the glory of nature, as found in California, struck a responsive chord in Worcester, who saw aspects of God's own nature in every leaf, bud, and outcropping.

Worcester's new congregation formally organized in 1870 and met at Druid's Hall on Sutter Street. Little is known about his activities during these early years. In 1877 Joseph quit the congregation, because, according to Alfred, he was dissatisfied with himself as a pastor and so insisted on surrendering his parish. He moved across the bay to Piedmont, where over the course of a year, January to December, 1877, he built a spacious house on land belonging to his cousin, Arthur Bowman. For the next ten years he lived alone in this house with a collie and, on one occasion at least, a Chinese servant. Worcester seemed to think of the isolated residence as "a good place for some sober thinking on my part" and a country retreat from city life for his occasional visitors.[73]

This house was Worcester's first known attempt at practicing architecture. While unsophisticated, it at least was utterly unlike the ubiquitous Italianate houses being built then for rich and poor alike. With its low profile, hipped roof, overhanging eaves, covered porch, exterior of unpainted shingles and interior of unpainted redwood, it may have qualified as the first consciously "rustic" house in the Bay Area. Indeed, it predated by a year or two the first shingle style houses built on the east coast by Henry Hobson Richardson and other architects. More important to Worcester, perhaps, was that the house did indeed seem to blend in with the open hillside. Piedmont was almost unpopulated then, and was very nearly in its natural state.

The house's influence upon local architecture was, at first, practically nil. Its lines were awkward, and its location was remote. Nevertheless, Worcester took great care in its design and was very pleased with the result. He adorned the house with vines and climbing roses, and planted fruit-bearing trees and bushes near the house.[74] Later the house began to be appreciated by people outside Worcester's circle of friends. Jack London, who lived there in 1902, loved the redwood interior and planted grounds, and thought the house "very, very comfortable."[75]

Worcester spent the next six years employed as a tutor of his cousin's children and others in Oakland. When he resumed the pastorate of the Church of the New Jerusalem in 1884, he commuted across the bay to do so. He appears to have kept up his studies in architecture during these years, if his surviving collection of architectural photographs and scrapbooks at the University of California is any indication.[76] In 1887 he lost his home. His cousin had gone bankrupt, and since Bowman had never gotten around to deeding Worcester's home site to him, the house went to Bowman's creditors. Worcester moved across the bay to 1407 Jones, from whence he planned his next project, the three shingled houses for Emilie and David Marshall.

There are no photographs, in Worcester's collection at the University of California, of the great early shingle style houses by eastern architects H. H. Richardson, Peabody and Stearns, Bruce Price, William Ralph Emerson, and McKim, Mead and White. These huge houses for wealthy clients were sprawling, asymmetrical structures with wings, towers, and porches built on suburban, country, or beachside lots. As picturesque as their shapes may have been, what really mattered about these houses, architecturally speaking, was

their exterior wall surface: a skin of smoothly flowing, evenly laid shingles which turned corners and filled every nook and cranny. Some of them rested on tall foundations of rough-cut stone, giving the house the appearance of rising up from the rock of the earth itself. Gone was the Victorian stickwork and the imitation medieval half-timbering which broke up the surface of houses, and gone was the abstract, "Eastlake" ornament which filled in these surfaces. By comparison, these new shingle style houses were infinitely more restful to look at. With their "natural" materials, one might say they were particularly well suited to their non-urban settings.[77]

In the Bay Area, only two shingle style houses were built previous to Worcester's experiment in the style. Both were designed by the great New York architect Bruce Price. The J. V. Coleman house at the northwest corner of Washington and Octavia streets was built in 1885 and, although the gables were decorated in Queen Anne-fashion, the rest of the house was covered with smoothly flowing shingles. In San Mateo, Price designed a larger and better house for George Howard, son of the Mexican-era and gold rush merchant W. D. M. Howard. George Howard went east to be educated and undoubtedly picked up a taste there for the latest architectural styles as well. He inherited his father's 6000 acre estate, The Uplands, and built his Bruce Price-designed house there in 1886.[78]

Not a single California architect seems to have been influenced by these two houses, or by the shingled houses on the east coast which were illustrated in *American Architect and Building News*, until after 1889, when a flood of shingled houses were built in San Francisco and Berkeley. As for Joseph Worcester, his influences remain unknown. Did he receive copies of *American Architect?* To what extent was he influenced by the designs of eastern architects in its pages and by the Coleman

Looking northwest from the Livermore residence toward 1034 and 1036 Vallejo. The fruit trees may have been planted by George R. Turner in the 1860s. Courtesy George Livermore.

house?[79] It seems likely that he was aware of these designs in 1888, but there remains the fact that he seems to have worked out his own Ruskinian-Swedenborgian design philosophy, and built his Piedmont house in a sort of crude shingle style, before any of the eastern shingled houses were built. Most likely he refined his personal ideas as a result of what was happening in the east. Certainly the houses he designed for the Marshalls showed advancement over his Piedmont residence.[80]

Construction began on the Marshalls' three houses in September or October, 1888, and the houses were most likely finished in January or February, 1889. Today, only two of the three houses, numbers 1034 and 1036 Vallejo, still stand today. Their status as the oldest shingle style houses in the Bay Area, and the first ever designed by a local figure, make them tremendously important as architectural icons.[81]

At first glance, they are not very prepossessing — they appear to be very simple shingled houses. Closer study reveals a sophistication in their design, especially as they relate to each other. The three houses were staggered in their relationship to the property line on Vallejo Street. The westmost house, #1036, was placed closest to the street, the next house, #1034, was set back on the lot a slightly greater distance, and the eastmost house, #1032, was set back farther still. This progression of setbacks forced the viewer to regard the three houses as individual structures in a dynamic, unified arrangement. The loss of one, #1032, has diminished the other houses, though not fatally.

That the three houses were almost identical further connected them visually. Slight differences in the fenestration, however, served to preserve their individuality.

Each of these houses was a far maturer

One of the David and Emilie Marshall houses, 1034 Vallejo. Designed by Joseph Worcester. Photo by author.

creation than Worcester's Piedmont residence of 1877. In that house, shingles did not serve much more of a purpose than to provide a wall covering and to promote a rustic feeling by virtue of their rough wooden texture. By 1888, however, Worcester had learned that shingles can be used to create a flowing wall surface which turns corners to wrap around a building. The effect is a unified skin treatment which is profoundly anti-Victorian in spirit, because Victorian houses use ornament and strips of wood ("stickwork") to break up the wall surface. From gable tips to foundations, the Marshall houses were strictly shingles, interrupted only by windows. These houses, even more than Bruce Price's shingled house in Pacific Heights, signaled the beginning of the end of the Victorian era in San Francisco architecture.

Finally, we should note that Worcester solved in an inspired manner the question of whether the overall effect of each house should be horizontal or vertical. The narrow width of the houses imply verticality, but the shingles line up in horizontal bands. Worcester chose to emphasize the horizontal aspect in the manner by which he lined up the windows and by having the second story of each house project over the first by a few inches. The resulting overhang separates the two stories with a strong horizontal line.

About seven months after the Marshall houses were built the Marshalls allowed Worcester to build his own house on a strip of land at the eastern edge of their lot. They gave Worcester a free lifetime lease on the property and it appears they also paid the cost of construction. In part this may have been their way of paying for Worcester's architectural services, but in all likelihood the main reason for their generosity was Emilie's gratitude to Worcester for his pastoral services, which he performed for decades without pay. Worcester received $900 per year from a family trust, and this was sufficient for his modest living expenses... but owning property was quite beyond his means. Worcester and the Marshalls, then, along with other members of the tiny Swedenborgian congregation, related to each other economically in what might be described as a barter system, but would be more accurately described as a communal spirit. Although the evidence is sparse, it appears that Worcester felt he had no choice but to serve his congregation as a pastor without pay. He also spent some of his own money on important causes, and in return he received gifts such as that of the Marshalls.[82]

Worcester's new house, 1030 Vallejo, was modest by almost any standard. It was smaller than the one he had had in Piedmont, but like

Looking northwest toward the Worcester-Marshall houses. Worcester's house, 1030 Vallejo, is at right. California State Library.

Looking north from the Livermore residence toward the Worcester-Marshall houses. The Worcester residence (1030 Vallejo) is at right, and the Marshall houses are to its left. Detail of a 1914 photo. Courtesy George Livermore.

it with its low profile and hipped roof.[83] Feeling that there was nothing of note to see to the south across Vallejo Street, Worcester placed the entrance on the west side of the house and the bay window on the east, facing the bay. The house was shingled on all sides, and the south wall, facing Vallejo, was a blank wall of shingles. Quite unlike the gabled, elongated Marshall houses in form, the Worcester house also broke with the staggered pattern established by them. Worcester's cottage came forward almost to the Vallejo Street property line. This meant that his residence did not impede 1032 Vallejo's eastward views of the bay, and it incidentally allowed Worcester to have a large back yard.

The construction of 1030-1036 Vallejo initiated a new social era on the Summit. By 1889 the gold rush crowd had all but vanished. Of the adults present on the Summit in the 1850s, only Maria Homer and Almarin Brooks

Paul remained — and Maria Homer would die in February, 1891, a year after Worcester's cottage was completed. To fill the void an artistically minded group of people — artists, writers, architects, and publishers — moved to the Summit beginning in 1889.

The first was Mary Curtis Richardson, a portrait painter who probably knew Worcester through his close friend, the artist William Keith. In the mid-1880s Mrs. Richardson rented studio space at 611 Clay Street, where Keith was also located. In all likelihood it was Keith who introduced Worcester and Richardson, leading to the latter's residence at 1032 Vallejo early in 1889, a year before Worcester was able to move into his own cottage.

Mary Curtis' infancy was adventurous. At age two she crossed the isthmus of Panama on the back of an Indian. This was in 1850, when Mary and her mother were traveling to California to join Mary's father. He became a

Thomas and Mary Curtis Richardson residence, 1032 Vallejo. California Historical Society.

Collector of Internal Revenue in San Francisco and was also a copper plate engraver. Both Mary and her sister Leila became interested in art by watching their father, so they were sent east for instruction in wood engraving in the 1860s. They returned to set up a studio and shop, with Mary doing the drawing and Leila as the block-cutter.

At age twenty-one Mary married Thomas Richardson, a Canadian in the lumber business. He supported her artistic interests, and her friends urged her to become serious about her painting, so she took instruction under Benoni Irwin, Virgil Williams, and William Sartain. She became a portrait artist, specializing in mother-and-child paintings and becoming known as the "Mary Cassat of the West." She won commissions in large numbers and was probably well-established by the time she and her husband moved to Russian Hill. After 1899 she frequently went east to do portrait work. Her exhibits traveled as far as New York, London, and South America, and she won occasional medals.

In her own words she sought, both in her work and life, "to get at the soul behind the mask of flesh" and to feel "a greater sympathy for people." After her death, a catalog of an exhibit of her paintings objectively noted:

> Mary Curtis Richardson was a born painter. She took so great a delight in color that she was sometimes carried away by it, and her pictures lack, perhaps, constructive elements, the absence of which she was the first to acknowledge and deplore. She showed also in the weakness of her time, a too great emphasis on sweetness and charm.[84]

In a work by her at the DeYoung Museum, however, what is most striking is the rich texture of the painted canvas, as well as the brilliant color. The portrait stands out vividly from across the room.

*   *   *

Their mutual friend, William Keith, never lived on Russian Hill, but in his visits to Worcester he became a frequent presence there.

Keith had known the Rev. Worcester since at least 1880, and probably longer, according to Keith's biographer, Brother Cornelius. At first their common bond was Worcester's interest in art. But when Keith's wife Elizabeth died in 1882, the artist was utterly desolated, and it was Worcester who was instrumental in pulling Keith out of his despair. The two were close friends thereafter.

Worcester took to visiting Keith almost daily at 11 a. m. at the latter's studio, and Keith, in turn, made a visit each Wednesday at noon to Worcester's cottage on Russian Hill, as soon as it was completed in about March, 1890. From Keith's downtown studio a cable car took him most of the distance, but muscle power was required for the last few, steep blocks. Whether at Keith's or Worcester's the talk centered most often on art, and the pastor had a strong influence on the artist's work. From a lighter, sunnier feeling, Keith moved into a dark, somber period which dominated his later years and during which he acquired his greatest fame. "Mr. Worcester was responsible for Keith's somber paintings, generally," stated aesthete Charles Keeler. According to Brother Cornelius, "Keith would put before his reverend friend bright and somber pictures, and Mr. Worcester, in his highly refined ladylike manner and voice, which Keeler imitated to a 'T,' would say 'Oh, I think that one, the dark one, is by far the better.'" Keith's somber, moody paintings could send Worcester into an aesthetic ecstasy. Once, when a man urged Keith to put more detail into a painting in progress, Worcester, also present, said "'Oh no, no, no, no!' — delicately holding up his gloved fingers — 'don't change a particle.'"[85]

In Brother Cornelius's opinion, Worcester "considered the technique, but even more the spirit that informed the technique of art."

Regarding this spirit, Worcester once informed Katherine Hittell, "If you wish to be a good and earnest creative writer, you must have more feeling for religion."[86] Writing, art, architecture — all acquired depth and meaning in similar ways.

Sometimes Mary Curtis Richardson would walk over from 1032 Vallejo to join Keith during his visits to Worcester's cottage, and sometimes Charles Keeler would be there. Keeler had gotten to know Keith upon buying one of his paintings, for Keith detected a sincere appreciation in the young writer who wanted a painting he could not really afford. And so Keeler, who later wrote *The Simple House* and helped found The Hillside Club of Berkeley (both of which promoted rustic, shingle style houses), joined the Worcester group that was forming on Russian Hill.

From various sources — photographs, written sources, and an architectural plan — we can recreate the interior of Worcester's house and describe the reception he gave his guests. In their writings, there is always a great deal of feeling as these visitors recall their host and his home, and a strong suggestion that the house itself was a reflection of Worcester's personality. Though humble and inexpensively built, the house seemed cozy and inviting to Worcester's friends.[87]

From Vallejo Street visitors ascended a few steps and entered a small garden around the front porch, on the west side of the house. The front door opened into a vestibule, whence one continued into the living room where Worcester entertained. This room was paneled entirely in waxed, hand-polished redwood. Directly opposite the bay window was a fireplace of

Joseph Worcester residence, interior. Note the redwood paneling and the fireplace, probably of buff-colored bricks. Courtesy Richard Longstreth.

buff-colored brick, where Worcester boiled water in his teapot, which hung on a wrought-iron swinging arm. He also warmed bread in the coals of this fireplace. Dark, somber paintings by Keith and portraits by Mrs. Richardson hung on the walls, and various items of interest, including a telescope by which one could make out ferryboat passengers, were placed about the room. A bunch of pinecones sat on the mantlepiece. His books were on philosophy, religion, literature, and poetry. There were three photographs of friends — John Muir, Professor LeConte, and Keith — also placed in view.

This living room (some visitors referred to it as a study) seemed somehow rather large, despite fitting into such a tiny cottage. In the northern half of the house were the dining room, bedroom, kitchen and bath.

"I'm the whole family," Worcester greeted one visitor from Massachusetts, who in turn wrote to one of Worcester's relatives: "Here he lives absolutely alone.... He does not look at all like the other Worcesters; he is tall and thin and angular with stiff self-conscious motions and a ready flash of inward smile, — the smile at some radiance of his own thought. He talks very little and very slowly, picking his words with care, and looks inward not outward as he talks."[88] The slender pastor, who usually dressed in black, had white hair and a well-trimmed white beard. His shoulders had a marked slope. The drawing of him which is printed here closely matches the descriptions of him from several sources.[89]

To his guests, Worcester served always the same refreshments. It was a modest menu, yet several friends were so appreciative that they

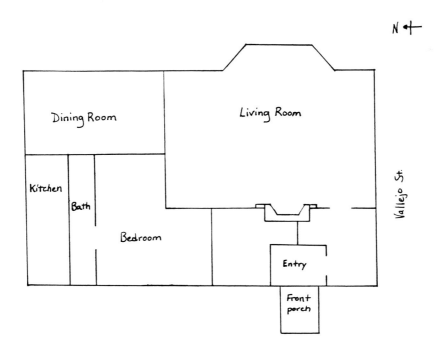

Plan of the Joseph Worcester residence, 1030 Vallejo Street. This drawing is roughly adapted from a plan drawn by Eldredge T. Spencer in 1945, omitting his addition on the north end of the house and an earlier addition of a window by Robert Boardman Howard. Documents Collection, Environmental Design Library, University of California.

took the trouble to record the simple fare. Charles Keeler's is the best description:

> And then the lunch! Never did French bread, warmed on the coals of the hearth, taste so good, with a huge pat of sweet, unsalted butter and a great pile of marmalade on the plate. Strong black tea, brewed on the coals of the hearth, completed the repast, and Mr. Worcester taught me to sweeten it with marmalade. Occasionally there were walnuts to crack and eat for dessert. It was a feast for the gods.

Everything was fresh and of the best quality. Sometimes Mrs. Richardson brought over some muffins, otherwise the menu was as described above. After the meal, the table was cleared, and a half-hour or so of conversation ensued. The unchanging procedure became something of a ritual, always looked forward to.[90]

Gradually the small number of friends became a large number of visitors, for Worcester was becoming popular. To conserve his time he rarely visited others, unless someone had need of him as a minister. His friend Edmund H. Sears wrote later:

> He had to resist many attempts to make him meet the world. Had he not done so he would easily have been overwhelmed with kindly attentions from those who wished to draw him into their own social sphere.... To all those who sought him out of spiritual need, the dwelling was freely open. Not only so, but to their own homes he would go with gladness whenever he could be of use. But others, if they wished to know him and share his thoughts, must climb the hill.[91]

Though reticent, he was congenial, and his welcome was apparently sincere. Naturally, he had his preferences. He liked alert, educated people, and was drawn to those with open and inquiring minds. He apparently got great satisfaction from conversations with people that probed a subject deeply and did not avoid hard questions. Nevertheless, he carefully considered the interests and limitations of his friends, and did not push them to talk about subjects outside of their interests.

Edmund Sears recalled his manner:

> He spoke always in a quiet even tone that put others at ease. If others spoke he listened with an almost deferential desire to know the thought the speaker would communicate. Were anything expressed that to his own thinking called for modification or correction, he would express disagreement, but so courteously as to avoid the appearance of offering rebuke. Quite surely and certainly, indeed, the disagreement would be expressed on any question of moral or grave significance that had called forth an opinion that should not, Mr. Worcester felt, go unchallenged....[92]

Sears felt that Worcester "brought into common daily converse a sincerity and a love of truth that lifted intercourse to what might be called an ideal plane." On the other hand, we should perhaps take Sears' panegyric with a grain of salt. Charles Keeler gives us a more three dimensional portrait:

> Shy as an inexperienced girl, reserved and restrained to an almost morbid degree, he was yet a determined fighter for his principles. Tall and slender, with a florid expression, he averted his eyes looking downward as he faced you, nevertheless there was in the man a quiet power that could move mountains. In his repressed suit of black, he stood before one as a personality of no ordinary type. His deep, low voice was full of emotion.[93]

Charles Murdock, the printer and Supervisor, remembered him this way:

He was painfully shy, and he was oppressed and suffered in a crowd....

He was essentially the gentle man. In public speaking his voice never rang out with indignation. He preserved the conversational tone and seemed devoid of passion and severity. He was patient, kind, and loving. He had humor, and a pleasant smile generally lighted up his benignant countenance. He was often playfully indignant. I remember that at one time an aesthetic character named Russell addressed gatherings of society people advising them what they should throw out of their over-furnished rooms. In conversation with Mr. Worcester I asked him how he felt about it. He replied, "I know what I should throw out — Mr. Russell." It was incongruous to think of the violence implied in Mr. Worcester throwing out anything that it provoked a hearty laugh.[94]

Once, Worcester met on the street a great, effusive magnate of the city whose grandson was in Worcester's Sunday school class. When thanked for his good work, the pastor replied, "What good can I do for the boy when at his grandfather's table he hears nothing but profanity!" By report, the profanity soon ceased.[95]

Really remarkable is the metaphoric impression Worcester left on several people: they thought he resembled Jesus Christ. Edmund Sears wrote of a woman who met Worcester briefly, and later told her companions in awe, "Why, he looks like Christ!" Brother Cornelius collected four such incidents, identifying each person who called Worcester "the most Christ-like man I ever saw," etc. George Livermore remembers that his father Norman had the same impression. Cornelius gave the matter thought and decided that it was not so much Worcester's appearance as his "reverent earnestness that inspired awe in those who saw him," which created the impression.[96]

The impression was not universal. One woman remembered his excessive reserve and a "shrinking and fawning manner." As a child, she said, "I shrank from him and his hand touch, which could not be called a hand clasp." And William Keith's second wife wrote, "It always seemed to me as though his desire to be sincere was almost morbid."[97]

Lincoln Steffens sorted through Worcester's various sides, tried to reconcile them, and formed his own opinion. Steffens found him

...an exquisite, very shy old bachelor gentleman who loved the city, which, somehow, understood him.... A New Englander and a Swedenborgian minister, he thought that he was moral and the town thought he was, but he was really an aesthete who saw and practiced and personified the Beautiful rather than the Good and the True. His tiny church [on Lyon Street] was a work of art, a temple to taste, set in a large, cool formal garden. The conflict of his culture and his instinct confused him. Standing on his hill one night, dressed as always in his well-cut, perfectly brushed and pressed long black clerical garb, he looked away from the bay down upon the red lights of Chinatown, Little Italy, and the Barbary Coast, and whispered, "Beautiful."

"But wicked," he added to me, after a long moment of silence. "It is very wicked. And, do you know, I think that that is why I love it so, this wicked, beautiful city.[98]

Another time, Steffens asked Worcester about two ex-convicts he had taken into his home. (Worcester's very remarkable work with ex-convicts and orphans will be discussed in a later volume.)

"Oh, they are gone," he flashed. "I caught them looking over some writings of mine on my desk. "

"So!" I said, "You forgive them burglary, but not —"

"Ah, but they must be gentlemen," he answered. "Even burglars. Like the strike, like the graft and the prosecution of grafters [this must have been in 1907] , like the wicked city itself — everybody and everything must be — understandable, beautiful; not ugly."

And having spoken as one having authority, this delicate arbiter of taste shrank back, down into his habitual mien of humility.[99]

Worcester could be rather sure of himself as he issued his advice — however delicately — and offered his opinions.[100] He was aware of his tendency to feel superior, and did not approve of it. Perhaps his humility was an affectation — a cloak to shield the world around him from his arrogance.

After witnessing a portion of the graft trial of 1907 with Lincoln Steffens, Worcester in a rather confused state told him,

"I — I am like those poor creatures in that court room. Secretly. And my sin is worse than theirs. It is conscious; it is conscious superiority. Do you know what I was saying to myself as I sat there listening to those witnesses? I kept saying, 'Well, I wouldn't do that; no, not that.'"

"But you wouldn't, would you?" [asked Steffens].

He looked astonished at me. He started to walk on, halted, and reddening a bit, he said: "I have never done any of the things they did. I have never been tempted to. But I have done similar things; I have done and I have left undone things that made those men in there do what they did. And I keep forgetting it."

He walked on, I with him for a block or two, when he lifted his face again to — almost moan, "I cannot — ever — get over my New England sense of superiority."

There was no smile. His face had gone white, whiter than his hair, against the fine black hat and coat. He meant it deeply.[101]

Looking south from the Marshall property, ca. 1904. Rev. Worcester's house is at left, and the Livermore residence is in the distance. Courtesy George Livermore.

Willis Polk

In 1889-1890, when the Richardsons and Worcester first came to the Summit, Russian Hill had long been bypassed in the eyes of most middle- and upper-class San Franciscans as a desirable place to live. Its housing stock was old and out of fashion, whereas thousands of spacious new houses with double parlors, servants' quarters, and modern amenities such as indoor plumbing and electricity were being built in Pacific Heights, the Western Addition, and the Mission district. All of the old neighborhoods, from Rincon Hill to Russian Hill, were "filtering down" to a less wealthy clientele. A sort of faded gentility still clung to the best of the early elite districts, thanks to some of the original residents who refused to move; and the houses were sometimes considered in a romantic light due to their connection with the city's early days; but home buyers sought modernity.

In this light it is hardly surprising that one of the Summit's old houses was virtually abandoned by 1890. When Peter G. Partridge lost his house at the southeast corner of Vallejo and Florence in 1879, it was purchased by one J. M. Wood, who was an absentee landlord for the next ten years.[103]

The house was next purchased in

Willis Polk. Documents Collection, College of Environmental Design, University of California.

December, 1889 by Horatio P. Livermore, an industrialist and manager of a wholesale drug firm. Livermore seems to have picked up the house as a sort of afterthought, perhaps as payment for debts owed to him. He certainly had no interest, then, in moving into the house from his family's large estate at Rockridge (Oakland). He may have hired a caretaker to live in the house. Many years later his widow told Brother Cornelius that, at about the time Worcester came to live on the hill, "the hill was far more bleak and the site of the later Livermore estate was occupied by a poor old Irish woman's shanty and strewn with rubbish — a paradise for goats" (Brother Cornelius's wording).[104] Though it was hardly a shanty, this must be a reference to the Morrison-Turner-

Partridge house, where the Livermores later lived.

The *Chronicle* columnist Edward Morphy painted a similarly decrepit picture when he told how the architect Willis Polk came to live in the house. The story is probably mostly inaccurate, but since Morphy's neighborhood histories are mostly truthful we shall repeat it for the record:

> Willis Polk and Emil Carlsen, the artist, discovered the place one night while they were rambling the hill in quest of inspiration. The house was deserted and had practically no window panes left unbroken.
>
> The small boys who fought each other on the adjacent vacant lot had seen to that; but it looked very beautiful in the moonlight and Willis decided then and there to live in it if he could.[105]

Polk then sought out Livermore (said Morphy), and Livermore, not wanting to fix the place up himself, let Polk have the place rent free if he would remodel it.

In truth, there was nothing so random about Polk's discovery of the Livermore house (as we shall call it hereafter). Polk had an architectural practice in partnership with Fritz Gamble, and the Gamble family was close friends with the Livermores.[106] They all lived in Oakland, and Polk undoubtedly met Horatio through his partner. While wholly speculative, this scenario presents itself: Livermore had an old house that he did not know what to do with. Polk, newly arrived in the Bay Area, and with a far from thriving architectural practice, was poor. Would he be interested in living in the house and improving it? Polk of course would have to see the place first; perhaps he did so at night, in company with Emil Carlsen.

Willis Polk moved into the ground floor of Horatio P. Livermore's house on Russian Hill sometime during December, 1890 to February, 1891.[107] He then met Joseph Worcester, and the results of this acquaintance became evident in Polk's remodeling of the Livermore house entry and living room. Redwood paneling, left in its natural state, covered the entire surface of these rooms, and a brick fireplace similar to Worcester's was placed in the west wall. The Swedenborgian minister seems to have made an architectural convert only a year after moving to Russian Hill. The act of homage would be repeated a little over a year later when Polk, his father, and his brother built their own house nearby in 1892.

One by one — first the Richardsons, then Worcester, then the Polks and others — a new community of like-minded people was moving to the top of Russian Hill. One of their common traits was a distaste for Victorian architecture, and for most of them the Summit, with its old housing stock essentially devoid of Eastlake millwork, decorative shingles, corner towers and useless belvederes, must have been an attraction. Far from following the fashionable trends of the time, these new residents would become tastemakers themselves. No one, in fact, was more determined to do so than Willis Polk.

Willis Polk — the *enfant terrible* of San Francisco architecture, the brash, outspoken critic, the stuntsman, the *bon vivant*, always broke. No one could have been less like Joseph Worcester in temperament. And yet the two became close friends, and mutual admirers. The secret to their friendship may be that Polk's love of beauty in architecture was as strong as Worcester's. Worcester preached beauty; Polk listened. (There were probably very few people that Polk listened to. His arguments with clients, for instance, are legendary.) Although Worcester never again, as far as is known, acted as an architect after designing his own cottage on Vallejo Street, his philosophy was disseminated through Polk and other architects who worked for decades to come.

Today it would be easy to assess Polk's early Bay Area work and, finding much of significance, conclude that he was a prominent architect within a few years of his arrival. In fact, few of Polk's early commissions were big ticket items, and he later expressed the opinion that it took him a very long time to achieve success. Polk felt belittled by the architectural establishment, and blamed his troubles on his haphazard training. Five years of formal instruction, he once said, would have saved him ten years of struggle.[108] Polk however, impatient to make his mark, consistently abandoned such training when it was available to him. He instead bounced around the continent, a few months here, a few there, picking up a wide range of influences in a short time. One must wonder whether rigorous instruction from a single source, as useful as it might be in matters of proportion and perspective, might have had a restricting effect on Polk's muse. He proved to be one of the more imaginative architects in San Francisco's history, and he had his proportion and perspective down, too.

In his book *On the Edge of the World* Richard Longstreth has thoroughly documented Polk's career from early apprenticeships in the mid-west through 1900, when Polk left Russian Hill. The young architect left an amazing trajectory for the future historian to piece together. Born in Illinois in 1867, Polk began working for a building contractor in St. Louis at age eight and went to work for his father, Willis Webb Polk, a builder of some note, in his teens. At age seventeen he became a partner with his father as W. W. Polk and Son, this time in Kansas City. He learned construction techniques and the rudiments of design and became an accomplished draftsman. In 1887, when not yet twenty, Polk forever left the world of Victorian design for a Romanesque and classical milieu by going to work as a draftsman for the prominent architects Van Brunt and Howe, late of Boston, and now moving to Kansas City. Henry Van Brunt stressed classicism and the academic training of his draftsmen, and employment here must have been invaluable to Polk. Yet in six months Polk was off to Los Angeles to work under Ernest Coxhead, then to Kansas City to work with his father briefly, and then to New York, where he attended classes at Columbia University. Somewhere in this itinerary was a trip to Washington D. C. In New York he worked for Charles Atwood (later head of design in Daniel Burnham's office) and then for A. Page Brown, who was attracting important commissions and had trained under McKim, Mead, and White. Here, Polk met the masters and saw much of their revolutionary work. Finally, when Mrs. Charles Crocker of San Francisco decided she wanted an eastern architect to design her husband's tomb, Brown, who got the job, moved his office to San Francisco, bringing Polk with him. As Longstreth points out, Polk had crossed the continent three and a half times in only two years.[109]

A. Page Brown instantly became *the* society architect of San Francisco, and accordingly attracted commissions for skyscrapers, churches, mansions, world's fair buildings, etc. A few years under Brown would have solidified Polk's credentials enormously. Nevertheless, in only a year Willis Polk, not yet twenty-three, left to open his own office.

He took as a partner Fritz Gamble, of a prominent Oakland family. Gamble had no training and little, if any, talent, but he did have social connections, a commodity of which Polk was in great need.[110] After six months, unfortunately, their only commissions were a pair of houses in Sausalito, where they were hardly noticed.

Polk then embarked upon a stunt designed to call attention to his existence to the

Willis Polk's 1890 remodeling of the Livermore residence, shown 1904. Courtesy George Livermore.

architectural fraternity and, hopefully, clients. This was a magazine, the *Architectural News*, the first issue of which appeared in November, 1890. Large format (9" x 13"), on fine paper, and beautifully designed, it was a remarkable accomplishment for a twenty-three year old who was new in town. If Polk's mission was to challenge the established *California Architect and Building News* as a beacon of good taste, the first issue showed he might succeed.[111]

Unlike *California Architect*, which primarily published designs by local architects in Victorian styles, Polk only ran illustrations which reflected the newer eastern trends and of old buildings in Europe. His choice of contributors, unfortunately, hardly varied from issue to issue — all were young friends of his, none particularly established — and some of the material was poor. Polk either failed or disdained to attract material from more

established architects. Polk folded the magazine after its third issue, apparently substantially in debt.[112] Still, he did achieve one objective: practically everyone in the Bay Area interested in architecture had now heard of him.

Polk continued to practice architecture with Gamble (if "practice" is the right word for the desultory nature of their business) for the three months of the magazine's existence and about seven months thereafter. Then, through his partner, Polk met good friends of the Gamble family, the Horatio P. Livermores. As a result, he moved into Livermore's vacant house on Russian Hill sometime during the winter of 1890-1891.

Polk quickly remodeled the first floor interior of his new residence. The result was utterly different from other interiors then being built on the west coast (in what we now call

Victorian styles), and Polk's work soon attracted comment from a society magazine, *The Wave:*

> Mr. Polk resides in a curious old house on the top of Russian Hill, commanding a panorama of bay and city quite unrivaled. Its interior he has fitted up in a curious and artistic way, converting the lower floor into one of the most interesting rooms in the city. Here he does all his own designing, drawing, and sketching.[113]

Polk's friend, the artist Ernest Peixotto, sensitive to the special qualities of Polk's work, wrote a better description in 1893:

> The room designed by Mr. Polk is finished throughout in large panels of redwood, dovetailed where the paneling is too large to be made of one board. The ceiling is supported by heavy beams, ornamented with delicate mouldings. His beautifully designed mantels and picturesque staircases are notable features of his interiors. His redwood is always left either in natural finish or simply waxed, so as to show the exquisite color and texture of the wood.[114]

Save for a fluted Doric column, also made of redwood, which gave the room a classical touch, the design resembled nothing so much as Joseph Worcester's living room just across the street.

Social events at Polk's new residence differed considerably from those at Worcester's. Polk socialized extensively with other young men who were climbing architects and businessmen, getting to know the world of fine restaurants and clubs. He became "known," and the newspapers and *The Wave* kept track of him more for his escapades than his architecture. In Oakland in 1890 Polk had hosted meetings of the Sketch Club at his home, which he called "Stagden." There, Polk, Ernest Coxhead, John Galen Howard, Fritz Gamble

and others met to party and discuss architecture.[115] In 1891-1892 a group of Bohemian Club members calling themselves the Roseleaves, dubbed by *The Wave* as "some of the wittiest men in San Francisco," met at the Livermore house with Polk as host and made the rounds of restaurants. Cigars, alcohol, musical instruments, formal dress, and an exclusively male membership characterized these frequent get togethers. In 1891 Polk designed (possibly gratis) a shingled, bungalow-type clubhouse for the Roseleaves, the Owl's Nest Club, in San Carlos, near the railroad station.[116]

Polk's practice remained desultory in 1891, with only four residential remodelings, the clubhouse, and one new residence built that year. Most important perhaps was his and Gamble's remodeling of the Boericke residence at 1812 Washington Street. Dr. Boericke was a parishioner of Worcester's Church of the New Jerusalem, and the commission was Polk's first in a prominently visible neighborhood. A striking new medieval, half-timbered facade was grafted onto the front of the old residence, and it provided the first evidence (aside from the Sausalito houses) to the general public that Polk could design in a historical mode on a par with A. Page Brown.[117]

Polk's career was given a needed boost when his family members moved to San Francisco from Kansas City in 1892. While there is no evidence that they lived with him in the Livermore house, there was room to spare there, and in all likelihood they joined him at 1023 Vallejo, as the house was numbered then. The family consisted of Willis Webb Polk, his wife Endemial Josephine ("Endie"), and their adult children, Dan and Daisy. The purpose was two-fold: Willis Webb would work as a building contractor in San Francisco, in partnership with the architects Willis Jefferson and Dan Polk; and the three men would build a family home on Vallejo Street, right next to

The Polk-Williams duplex, 1013-1019 Vallejo, early view. California State Library.

the Livermore house.

The new residence was actually built as half of a common-wall duplex, the other half belonging to Dora Norton Williams. Dora Williams was the widow of the landscape artist Virgil Williams, who had also been the founding director of the San Francisco Art Association's School of Design.[118] Although she was an artist herself, little is known about her painting. She is probably best known today for this house and for her close friendship with Robert Louis and Fanny Stevenson.

Endie Polk and Dora Williams each purchased lots in 1892 from one Spencer Brown, the absentee owner of the Ranlett house and the 50-vara lot that it sat upon. When Brown sold lots to Mrs. Polk (20' of frontage) and Mrs. Williams (40') it was the first time any of the four lots east of Florence Street had been subdivided. Though the Polks had the smaller lot, theirs was the one on the east, so they had

far better views of the city than Dora Williams had.[119] (The address then was 1015 Vallejo for the Polk side and 1019 Vallejo for the Williams. Today, as flats, the Polk side is #1013-1017.)

With its shingled exterior and natural redwood interior the Polk-Williams duplex continued the trend begun by Worcester. Willis Jefferson Polk, in his design of the house, now added a new dimension borrowed from historical precedent. As Longstreth has shown, the house closely resembled late-medieval, urban houses in Brittany, France.[120] Each side of the duplex was gabled, with flaring eaves; a Gothic arched window was inserted into the Williams gable; and shingles were used in decorative diamond patterns on the Williams side. On the Polk side, successive stories overhung lower ones. Other aspects of the duplex were anything but medieval. Horizontal bands of casement windows stretched across the duplex on the first and

Upper stories of the Polk residence, 1013-1017 Vallejo. Photo by author.

Upper stories of Dora Williams' residence, 1019 Vallejo. Photo by author.

Interior of Polk residence, attic story, early view. Courtesy George Livermore.

second stories, and the Gothic arched window in the Williams gable was nearly all glass, divided into twenty-two lights by delicate muntins. True to the spirit of the late-nineteenth century historical revivals, as pioneered by Henry Hobson Richardson and McKim, Mead and White, the Polk-Williams duplex was a modern adaptation of a medieval theme, one that lost nothing in the way of composition or detailing.

From Vallejo Street the duplex was a conventional two stories in height. It was built on an extremely steep slope, however, and in the rear the building spilled down the hillside with four basement levels, making the duplex, from top to bottom, six stories in height. Open balconies in the rear added an outdoors element to the building. The result was a substantial amount of living space fit onto narrow lots at a modest cost. The Polks had been creative in their exploitation of the steeply sloping property.

Indoors, the gable level of Mrs. Williams residence had a cathedral-like feeling with its open ceiling and Gothic window. Four pairs of casement windows directly below the gable flooded the interior with light. On the Polk side an open space two stories in height connected the living hall with a sort of studio loft. A balustrade with slender, turned posts ran the circumference of the opening and a wooden clock of Palladian design was set in the chimney above. The Polks had four fireplaces, one made of terra cotta panels, and three made of buff-colored bricks. These brick fireplaces were very similar to the fireplace in the Worcester house and to that in the Livermore house as remodeled by Polk. Everywhere the redwood paneling lent a feeling of warmth to the two residences. On the Polk side, there was a strongly vertical feeling as one climbed from one story to the next on narrow stairways.

To commemorate the vertical design of this house on the summit of the hill, a house

which looked down on the city below, the Polks inscribed a legend on one of the panels: *"Was Kummerts Den Mond das de Hunde Bellen?"* It translates roughly as "What does the moon care that the hound howls below?" expressing a Bohemian attitude common to the young Willis and his friends.

The duplex, then, was a remarkable synthesis of the east coast shingle style, medieval Brittannic urbanism, Joseph Worcester's love of natural materials, hilltop Bohemianism, and Willis Polk's creative genius.

Construction on the duplex proceeded swiftly, and it appears both residences were in move-in condition by October. Interior finishing of the Polk side continued into 1893. For the elder Polks this appears to have been their final residence, while for young Willis the next eight years would be a period of varying fortunes leading ultimately to the prominence he craved.

Bohemia followed Willis Polk into his new family home. The *Chronicle* columnist Edward Morphy described the Roseleaf parties as follows:

> There Dan Polk would play the banjo and Nealy O'Sullivan would sing; there Dan O'Connell would recite 'Roger and I' and tell the latest tales from Bohemia. Thither Charles Rollo Peters from his studio at the northwest corner of Taylor and Green, and Petey Bigelow from wherever he happened to be, and all the other artists and writers of the day.[121]

Polk helped to form another group with a more serious purpose the following year. He, Bruce Porter, A. Page Brown, Douglas Tilden, Arthur Mathews and others founded the Guild of Arts and Crafts on the principles of William Morris. They sought to offer advice on how to conduct architectural competitions and proposed a civic board for approval of municipal art projects. Polk and Porter also

Two early views of the interior of the Polk residence, top story. Courtesy George Livermore.

used the Guild to promote their idea of erecting a Robert Louis Stevenson monument in Portsmouth Square. Although the Guild soon disbanded, the Stevenson monument was ultimately created, with sculpture by Porter and a base by Polk.[122]

Polk's architectural career naturally improved with his father in town. His father seems to have had the ability to land building contracts, and Polk was able to work as architect on some of these projects. While little is known about Dan Polk's contributions, it should be noted that he was a first rate draftsman.[123] The partnership was formalized in October, 1892. As the *Chronicle* noted, "Willis Polk the architect has two partners, his father W. W. Polk, and his brother, Dan Polk. The firm name has not been decided on, but may be Polk, Polk, and Polk."[124] They decided on simply "Polk and Polk."

The firm was busy during 1892-1894 with about fifteen new residences, three residential alterations, a Mill Valley church, and a commercial building to their credit (besides the family home) during those years. At least a few of these were built by Willis Sr. With these commissions, Willis Jefferson Polk had an opportunity to display his facility with several styles based on historic precedent, including Venetian Gothic, Monterey (Mexican-era) revival, English cottage, classical revival, shingle, and Italian Renaissance. None of these was a literal copy from a historical period; rather, each was a free-wheeling adaptation for modern times, with impeccable compositions and proportions. The largest of these was the George Gibbs house at 2622 Jackson Street, in Pacific Heights. Built out of stone, this Italian palazzo attracted very favorable attention, not only for its size and building material, but for the restraint and dignity of its design. This is not the place to discuss Polk's architectural career in any detail; suffice to say that while still in his twenties he had exhibited

considerable sophistication on projects throughout the Bay Area.

The escapades did not stop with the blossoming of his career. Quite the opposite. In August, 1892, as the Polk-Williams duplex was nearing completion, Polk began his career as a journalist. A Southern Pacific train in the San Joaquin Valley was robbed by the notorious bandits Sontag and Evans while Polk was aboard, and when Polk jumped from the train he was bludgeoned in the face with a shotgun. At the next station he telegraphed an exclusive to the *Examiner*, for which he received cash and a walking stick. Remarked *The Wave*, "He is exhibiting the remnants of the check, the walking stick, and the scar to everyone on Kearny Street, between the hours of four and five, eight times a week."[125]

The Evans and Sontag episode followed Polk to his new abode on Russian Hill. Polk's friend Petey Bigelow tracked the two bandits down at their hideout in Visalia and interviewed them. This was closer than the Fresno County sheriff was able to get, so in frustration the sheriff followed Bigelow to San Francisco with a warrant for his arrest. Petey sought sanctuary with Willis Jr., and so up to 1015 Vallejo the sheriff tracked him. Bigelow fled from the back entrance while Willis Sr. answered the door. "Are you Willis Polk?" asked the sheriff. Answering truthfully in the affirmative, he was then arrested by the sheriff for harboring a fugitive from justice. Word got out that the sheriff had arrested the wrong Willis Polk, and so the lawman returned to Visalia, a laughingstock and emptyhanded.[126]

The *Call* newspaper recorded Willis Jr.'s altercation with the Holland nobleman Baron W. E. J. Van Belveren in July, 1893. It seems the two had attended a party of Bohemian and University clubmen at the Hotel San Rafael when, amid much drinking and dice playing, the Baron felt compelled to ask Polk whether he had been spreading rumors about him among society. Polk, confused as to his meaning, thought the Baron was accusing him of cheating at dice. In response the Baron declared, according to the *Call*, "'This insult can only be wiped out with blood, young Mr. Polk,' with withering emphasis on the adjective." The "son of Kentucky" (Polk liked to fancy he had been born in that state) readily expressed his willingness to meet the nobleman on the field of honor.

The next day, a sober Polk reflected upon the European background of his foe and began to feel horribly outclassed. In some desperation he obtained a pistol and began target practice in advance of the appointed hour. Who should happen by but the Baron, who observed Polk coolly (as he thought) drilling bullseyes as a warmup to the main event. Both men were so fearful that they allowed women friends to talk them out of the duel. They ended up drinking champagne to the other's health and threw dice to see who would pay the bill.[127]

There was the time Polk, who was very short, challenged Kreling to a wrestling match at Tait's and got dunked in the restaurant's fountain. There was the time he dressed as a woman to lampoon the suffragettes.[128] But while Polk's mind was sometimes distant from architectural matters, it was never so for very long.

In 1892 he began a series of articles on architectural criticism for *The Wave*.[129] In these he reviewed new and old buildings as a way of expounding his design theories. He praised the old Colton mansion by S. C. Bugbee on Nob Hill and the new Hibernia Bank at Jones and McAllister, by Albert Pissis. The entire Western Addition earned his contempt, and he made a series of jabs at Frank Shea's attempts to design a tower for the incomplete City Hall.

Sometimes the regular newspapers printed his opinions verbatim. In the *Call* Polk expressed his dissatisfaction with the plans for the Midwinter Fair and called for a Spanish renaissance style for the buildings. These would be based on the old missions, which after all were "the only pure style of art we [Californians] can lay any claim to" — although they should be more ornate. A very fine drawing by Polk of a Spanish window was included in the article.[130]

Three days later the same paper printed Polk's embarrassing comments on the City Hall tower. Shea's design had also been criticized by Wright and Sanders, and by Pissis, but Polk let out the stops: "The proposed tower is certainly bad... and any architect who would invent such a composition is architecturally incompetent." Polk suggested a jury of architects to judge such projects. However, "Such a thing would be impossible in San Francisco," Polk thought, "because the entire tribe of so-called architects is responsible for the hideousness of Market Street, the Western Addition, and all parts of the city except the Latin Quarter or the old part. [Mayor Ellert] should pull a string and precipitate all these architects from the commission's rooms to the bottomless pit. If such a lovely result could be obtained, I would gladly sacrifice myself among the herd."[131] Needless to say, such pronouncements did nothing to endear Polk to the more established architects of the city.

Polk's practice suffered a slowdown in 1895, with only three commissions in that year. (One of these, though, was for the William Bourne mansion at 2550 Webster, a blend of classical revival and Tudor styles built out of clinker brick, and one of Polk's surviving masterpieces.) In 1896 Polk received no known commissions whatever, save for the design of the bases of the Stevenson and Admission Day monuments. The cause of this slowdown in unknown, though Willis Webb Polk's serious illness of 1895-1896 probably contributed.[132]

Addison Mizner, who worked for the Polks for almost no pay during this period, and lived with them in their house, remembered that they were so poor they were reduced to fishing with a rope for lumber from an adjoining lot and hauling it up to burn for fuel.[133] The fact that Willis Jefferson continued to live in high style did not help matters, and the situation came to a head in 1896.

After a sojourn with Society at the Hotel Del Monte in August, 1896, Polk found himself unable to pay his bill of $50, and ignored several requests by the hotel for payment. As a result he was hauled into court by Judge Groezinger for a little half hour quiz. At the beginning of the interview Polk was evasive: he had no property, nor any credits; his only job in hand had been paid in advance, and the money was long since spent. When asked whether any judgments were outstanding against him, Polk, according to the *Call*, blurted out, "Yes, twenty or thirty of them, but they don't bother me a little bit. My business is designing buildings, not paying attention to lawyers."

An attorney for the hotel asked to see the books of Polk and Polk, in hopes they would show solvent credits due the firm. Polk however pleaded his father was ill and in Pasadena, and that he (WJP) had not kept books for eight months.

"We would like to have the books in court, Your Honor," said the attorney.

"I don't know where they are. I don't propose spending the time to look for them."

"Books or jail," said the judge, "by Monday next, 10 a.m." Then Polk "slammed his jaunty straw hat on his head and bolted out of court, vowing that he would go to jail first."

Five days later the *Call* reported that Polk had paid his bill, and that Collector Rauer promised to present more claims against Polk soon. Within a few days other creditors of Polk were encouraged by these events to file executions of judgment against him.[134]

One year later Polk's insolvency made the news again. In an article entitled "Short Memory of a Young Man About Town in Regard to Money Matters," the *Call* newspaper related that Polk now owed H. S. Crocker and Co. $1500 for goods sold and delivered, and $180 to Mrs. Willis Webb Polk for three months rent![135] The newspaper's assertion that Polk had no contracts in hand at the moment was not quite true; he had one. This was for the office building and residence of William Bourne's Original Empire Mine Co. in Grass Valley (both extant). The stone residence was another brilliant adaptation by Polk of historical themes, with vague references to old English cottages and to the Tudor style blended in a composition that was all Polk's.[136] This was his only commission for 1897. It seems William Bourne was largely responsible for keeping his friend Polk alive during the mid-1890s.

With relatively few commissions during his Russian Hill years, Polk had spare time to devote to other projects, some of which were quite interesting. As noted above, he and Bruce Porter promoted the construction of the Stevenson monument in Portsmouth Square, which they designed with George Piper. Numerous other speculative projects emerged from Polk's Russian Hill studios during the 1890s. In 1891 the *Examiner* published Polk's proposed plan for a Marina District and North Beach World's Fair, and in the same year an architectural journal published Polk's conception of an Examiner Building at Third and Market. In 1897 Polk dreamed up an unsolicited design for an arch and peristyle which would billow out from the front of the Ferry Building, which was then under construction. The result would have been a grand, semicircular civic plaza which streetcars and pedestrians would pass through on their way to the ferries. Although self-promotional impulses may have generated this project, it is also evidence of Polk's selfless interest in civic beauty, a trait he exhibited numerous times in later years.[137]

The city of San Francisco evidently

fascinated Willis Polk greatly. Although he professed to despise so much of the city — those districts built up during the 1870s and 1880s — he often celebrated it with drawings of the view from his Summit studio or from other vantage points. Whether quick sketches or carefully detailed delineations, these drawings are wonderfully evocative of the city's atmosphere and capture the sublimity of a city built on hills and seen through occasional fog. In 1894 seven of his sketches were used to illustrate an *Examiner* mood piece, "The City of St. Francis."[138] In 1900 he drew scenes of the Ferry Building and of the downtown area as seen from Nob Hill.[139] Shimmering and impressionistic, these drawings bore little resemblance to the crisp architectural renderings Polk did for pay. They paid homage to a city he was devoted to improving, and sometimes to preserving as it was.

Professionally, Polk was virtually idle again in 1898, but he did receive several commissions in 1899. His break came in 1900. The firm of Percy and Hamilton had long been one of the most important in the city. Designers of great industrial and civic projects, and pioneers in the use of reinforced concrete, they had also kept pace with changing times, adopting the classical revival style with facility and making the transition to the steel frame era in high-rise construction. When F. F. Hamilton died in December, 1899, the surviving partner, George Washington Percy, invited Polk to join the firm. Wary, perhaps, of Polk's ego, Percy declined to make Polk a partner, but he put Polk in charge of design and the firm became known as Percy and Polk.[140] A wave of important commissions now came Polk's way — a skyscraper, a warehouse, several commercial buildings, residences, etc. Polk received as much paid work in 1900 as he had in the previous several years combined.

He married Christine Barreda, daughter of a Spanish ambassador, that year and moved into the Barreda family home in Pacific Heights. In 1901 he moved to Chicago to join Daniel Burnham's firm, a move arranged in part by Joseph Worcester. After two years with Burnham, Polk returned to San Francisco, and after 1906 he became important in the rebuilding of San Francisco.

Willis Webb Polk died in about 1903.[141] His son Dan tried his hand at vaudeville, moved to New York to work briefly for McKim, Mead and White, and died, as Longstreth describes, "in almost total obscurity" in 1908.[142] In about 1902 Daisy and Endie Polk split their house into three flats; soon afterward Daisy married and the house became rental units. Polks never again lived on the Summit, but apparently Willis Polk never forgot it, either. During the mid-1910s he worked for Horatio and Norman Livermore on two major Summit projects that will be discussed in a later volume. More than even the Polk-Williams duplex, these later projects have been responsible for helping to define the architectural character of the Summit as we know it today.

Polk-Williams residence, 1013-1019 Vallejo, between 1906-1915. California State Library.

The Worcester Group

Dear Willis:

I am home from a day at the Blaney house and must tell you that it is a straight piece of enchantment. Exterior and interior are beautiful beyond any expectation of mine or theirs (or yours?) and somehow as I walked around and through the house it seemed to me a fulfillment of all the things that Mr. Worcester used to find in your art, and I could hear his chuckle of pleasure in my ears as I moved from one surprise to another. Somehow, being old and weary of art, the house gave me satisfaction that I have not felt for years and thought I could never recover. It is not, in any aspect, an imitation or affectation. You merely picked up the spirit of the early spontaneous Italian work, and made it your own, bring[ing] to it a sober romantic playfulness and poetry that is the very best of you, and that somehow, miraculously, brings in the Blaneys and all of us. The house might have been there forever, or it might after all be only a dream. It strikes me as the most enchanting structure I've ever seen and therefore may not be there when I go back.

Yours always,

B. P.

Bruce Porter to Willis Polk, letter, May 21, 1917, re: Polk's design of the Blaney residence in Saratoga, California[143]

Joseph Worcester was well aware of the less attractive aspects of Willis Polk's character, but it did not seem to matter much to the minister. Polk made a point of behaving in Worcester's presence, and the pastor may have been charmed by Polk's quick wit and exuberance. An anecdote illustrates Worcester's attitude. Someone once went to Worcester with the latest tale of Polk's excesses in hopes that the pastor could do something to reform him. Worcester replied, "If I had seen him do as you say, I might venture to admonish him but he has never shown that side to me; and on mere hearsay I cannot speak to him."[144]

With Polk's arrival at the Livermore house, the meetings of artists at Worcester's was expanded to include the architects Polk knew. Later others made their way to the pastor's cottage as well. The Worcester group now included Mrs. Richardson, William Keith, Polk, Bruce Porter, Ernest Coxhead, John Galen Howard, and Charles Keeler. Walter Bliss and William Faville are known to have joined them upon their return to San Francisco in 1898, after working under McKim, Mead and White in New York. Possible visitants include Bernard Maybeck (a friend of Keeler's), A. Page Brown, A. C. Schweinfurth, and John Muir, but of their presence at Worcester's there is no record. Muir disliked visiting the city, and Brown generally moved in wealthier circles.

Bruce Porter was a friend of Worcester's by 1894, probably much earlier, and he remained close to Worcester until the latter's death. As a child he had been taken to see Worcester's Piedmont house soon after it was built. Much later, in 1951, he told an interviewer that young architects went to Worcester for advice, and that "it was to him that they owed their thorough grounding in good taste and simplicity" (in the interviewer's words).[145]

Charles Keeler met Worcester through Keith in 1892. This founder of Berkeley's Ruskin Club and initiator of the Hillside Club probably absorbed much of Worcester's architectural philosophy (as well as Bernard Maybeck's) and expounded it through his own book, *The Simple Home* (1904).

Another architect should be mentioned *in absentia*: Daniel Burnham. He was a distant in-law of Worcester's (Burnham's brother Lewis was married to Alice Worcester, a niece of Joseph's), and the two had been friends for far longer than Worcester had known any of the people mentioned above. Burnham's family had moved to Waltham, Massachusetts in 1863, when he was seventeen, and they attended the Swedenborgian church there headed by Joseph's father. There, Burnham and Worcester became friends for life.[146] The two had occasion to meet several times during 1902-1905, when Burnham was in San Francisco to work on the Burnham Plan for the city.[147]

There is little in the way of description of these meetings of architects at Worcester's, but the indications are that Worcester, who had less training and experience than almost anyone, acted more as a teacher than as an equal participant. Keeler wrote that Worcester's "word was law in the select group of connoisseurs of which he was the center."[148] The Bruce Porter letter to Polk, which heads this section, shows that several years after Worcester's death his teachings were still on the minds of his friends. And Burnham, in a letter to William Keith, wrote of Worcester, "So much of the best I am able to know and particularly understand has come out of our long and dear friendship."[149]

Worcester and the Swedenborgian Church

To try to define Worcester's design philosophy would be hazardous, since he wrote little on the subject which survives. That he preferred simplicity over ornateness is clear enough; likewise that he was attracted to natural wood surfaces rather than stained or painted wood. Whenever possible he preferred a rustic or gardened setting. Beyond this, he apparently had very specific, well thought out ideas regarding detailing, composition, color, etc. His ideas were essentially religious in their basis, for he believed that God is manifest in nature, and architecture should therefore emulate nature. Both Charles Keeler and Willis Polk wrote at length regarding their ideas on architecture, and the reader is free to try to detect the teachings of Worcester in these (particularly in Keeler's *The Simple Home).* A more profitable method of discerning Worcester's architectural philosophy might be to visit the Swedenborgian Church at 2107 Lyon Street.

Built during 1894-1895, the church was a collaborative effort between A. Page Brown, the architect of record, Brown's assistant A. C.

Schweinfurth, Worcester, and several of the latter's friends. *Scientific American* credited Worcester with working closely with Brown,[150] and other evidence indicates that Worcester was closely involved with every step of the process. A friend of the Worcester family from the east who visited in 1901 went further: the church, according to Richard Cabot, was "Worcester's personal expression of himself." The arrangement of the church, indeed "each shrub and flower," was done with distinct choice and meaning.[151] It was Worcester who went to the Santa Cruz Mountains to select madrone trees for roof supports, and Worcester who instructed the brick masons to apply a downward slant to the mortar pointwork (still visible) so that each brick would cast a distinct shadow.

Worcester wanted the church to have a quiet, somber effect, like his homes. In advance of the actual design he wrote that, contrary to the ideas of his "artist friends," "I hope our plan will not be too aesthetic... a pretty church I do not think I could stand. I prefer the congregation in the bare hall."[152] The result is close to what he hoped for.

The garden adjoining the church may also have been Worcester's idea. His friend Cabot wrote in 1901 that Worcester "has so arranged it that you cannot enter the church, and can hardly see even the outside of it, until you have gone through a garden — the quietest and greenest imaginable."[153]

Worcester's friends contributed, too, Bruce Porter with two stained glass windows, and William Keith with four paintings. The chairs have been variously attributed to Maybeck, Schweinfurth, and Brown. Porter is consistently credited with having supplied the sketch or photograph of a church in northern Italy from which the campanile was modeled.[154]

The overall effect was captured in words by Richard C. Cabot, Worcester's visiting friend from the east: "It is a place where you sit down and have no desire to go away, a marvelously calming, reflective place, sending you in, and back in time and away to thoughts and plans you haven't seen in years."[155]

The church is small, and that was good, for Worcester's voice would have been lost in a larger space. He spoke in a soft monotone, as he did not believe in forcing his opinions on others at a church service. As Alfred Worcester wrote, "with never uplifted eyes he read his sermon. His voice from the pulpit was not what it was from the fireside. He seemed determined to eliminate from it every pleasing sound; but his reverence in reading from the Bible lessened the harshness of his preaching voice. His extreme self-abnegation, however, almost defeated his purpose, for his unconventionality was itself conspicuous."[156] His friend Charles Murdock added, "He was not attractive as a preacher, his voice trembled with emotion and bashfulness, and he read with difficulty."[157] This, the man whose personal magnetism drew so many to the Summit of Russian Hill!

A regular attendee of the church service was the artist William Keith, who took the ferry over from his Oakland home each Sunday to do so. He always sat at the rear of the church, by the fireplace, in a deep meditative state, nodding slowly to the drone of Worcester's sermons. He was too far away to make out the pastor's soft voice, but attended because "it does me good just to hear his [Worcester's] voice."[158]

Worcester rarely discussed Swedenborgianism in his daily life, at least, not among those who did not share his religion. He did give Keith some books on the subject early in their friendship, but the artist read them more out of friendship than conviction. Worcester, concluded Brother Cornelius, "disseminated more 'Joseph Worcesterism' than 'Swedenborgianism.'" Even his sermons touched only upon the more accessible aspects of the religion.[159]

However, when Richard Cabot visited Worcester in 1901, the two discussed religious symbolism, a special interest of Swedenborg's, "and we got intimate in a few sentences. I suppose he has not many acquaintances who jump at the chance to talk religion as we do, and though we did not finish the working out of our differences, we felt a very deep oneness of spirit with him."[160]

Kate Atkinson, Gelett Burgess, and Les Jeunes

"We demolished Decadence and picked Hope out of the dust-heap"

Sundial, Atkinson-Paul residence.
From Kate Atkinson, *The Home.*

Worcester and his circle formed only one of the artistic groups that met on the Summit during the 1890s. There was another just as active, and it centered around members of the Unitarian Church, particularly Kate Atkinson, Frank Gelett Burgess, and Bruce Porter. In the mid-1890s their activities began to attract wide notice, not just from San Franciscans, but nationally.

Relatively little is known about Kate Atkinson, and we shall soon have to turn our attention in this chapter to her neighbor, the writer, artist and publisher Gelett Burgess. Nevertheless, it is clear that Atkinson was the one who first drew Burgess and his group, *Les Jeunes*, to Russian Hill.

Kate Atkinson had been born in Ohio in 1845 and was old enough when she moved to California with her parents, in the early 1850s, to remember the event as an adult. She was eight when 1032 Broadway was built by her father Joseph. Upon his death in 1880 she inherited the house and continued living there with her aunt and uncle, Kate and Almarin B. Paul; their children, Jane, Florence and Almarin Jr.; and another uncle, John Mullen. All except Almarin Jr. lived at 1032 Broadway for the remainder of their lives.

A neighbor of Kate Atkinson and the Paul sisters remembered in 1977 that the three women "always seemed comfortable and came from wealth,... had good incomes and important social positions."[161] Kate Atkinson's wealth came mainly from one source: large parcels of land in the Presidio Heights district that her father had purchased in the 1850s, most likely from William H. Ranlett. Kate held on to this property until the district began to be settled in the 1890s, and of course by then the land was vastly more valuable.[162] Income from the sale of this property enabled her to travel widely and lead a highly cultured life.

Although she never had to work, it does not appear that she was content to coast on her father's investments and lead a life of leisure. There are scattered references to her activism and volunteer social work over the decades... references found in serendipitously discovered and preserved sources. In 1870 she worked energetically as a suffragette, serving as the secretary of the Women's Suffrage Association of San Francisco and as a delegate to their state convention.[163] In 1886-1887 she was the secretary of the Pioneer Kindergarten Society, one of several organizations in the city devoted to teaching and positively influencing juveniles who lived in rough neighborhoods and had marginal family lives. She was the Society's secretary again during 1896-1897, when it had three kindergartens (two South of Market and

Kate Atkinson. Courtesy Mrs. Arthur A. Moore.

one in the Barbary Coast).[164] She may have been active in other such efforts which remain unknown.

It appears that the Atkinson and Homer families were members of the Unitarian Church beginning in the 1850s. Our evidence for the early years is restricted to a newspaper report of Kate's recitation of a poem, "Young America," in a program of the church's Pioneer Sunday School in 1858; and while this is no proof that she was a member continuously, she did begin renting a pew at the new Unitarian Church at Geary and Franklin streets in 1890. Her neighbor Maria Homer was a member from at least 1870 (probably earlier) until her death in 1891, and Maria's daughter and grandchildren, the Parkers, were also members. Unitarianism appears to have been an important element of the Summit's history since the decade it was first settled.[165]

Frank Gelett Burgess joined the San Francisco church in 1890. Then twenty-four, Burgess worked as a surveyor for the Southern Pacific Railroad and had been transferred to the Bay Area by that company only recently. He quickly became active in the church's social activities and became someone that everyone knew. Within a year or so, thanks to his new friends in the church, his social orbit began to revolve more and more around the Russian Hill neighborhood.

Today no one thinks of Gelett Burgess as a railroad surveyor, nor as a college instructor in civil engineering, which was his next position. When they think of Burgess, they think of his poem "The Purple Cow," his drawings of Goops, his little magazine *The Lark*, and his romance novel, *The Heart Line*. Burgess plainly was not cut out for serious work, and when he finally admitted this to himself and concentrated on nonsense, he did a lot better. Spontaneous creativity was his métier, and while his act wore thin at times, from the comfortable distance of a century we can find much to love in Gelett Burgess.

He was born in Boston, Massachusetts in 1866, as Frank Gelett Burgess. (The blend of his conservative New England background, which he rebelled against, and his assertively nonsensical nature would someday produce curious results.) His parents were Unitarian, and his father Thomas had sailed on the whaling ship *Arctic* for four years under Captain William Gelette, for whom Burgess was named.[166] As a little boy he played in the streets of the South End and made a game of traversing as many blocks as possible through alleys or other mid-block routes, rather than on main streets. He was small in frame and sometimes bullied by Irish boys.

In high school and college he showed some of the traits and interests which would mark his life in California. He wrote poetry and prose and experimented with the theater, a printing press, and hashish. At MIT, where he studied civil engineering, his grades were poor, for he was often distracted by whimsy and adventure. He was part of a group called the "Foul Fiends of Hell," and kept a notebook called "Les Vagaries de Mon Esprit." He read widely — Hugo, Voltaire, Tolstoy, Montaigne, Dickens, Emerson, Scott, Eliot, Lewis Carroll — and liked to adapt couplets from his reading to better match his own taste, such as this one from Dryden:

> There is a pleasure in being mad
> Which none but madmen know.

One of his own invention read:

> A little nonsense now and then
> Is relished by the wisest men.

He worked as a topographer and surveyor in college, and upon graduation he went to work for the Southern Pacific Railroad,

Gelett Burgess, 1896. Gelett Burgess
Collection, Bancroft Library.

in San Francisco in 1865 to a Unitarian family; his father, Charles B. Porter, worked as a journalist. Bruce became interested in the arts, and he opened his own decorating and stained glass studios about a year after meeting Burgess. For some time his income was probably quite low, and throughout the nineties he lived with his parents at 1922 and 1924 Baker Street. He had strong romantic leanings, idolized Robert Louis Stevenson, affected a Stevensonian haircut and moustache, and draped his lanky frame with black clothes. During the nineties he was perhaps the only person who moved freely among the different artistic groups in town — Worcester's circle, *Les Jeunes* of Gelett Burgess, and the George Sterling crowd at Coppa's restaurant.

Burgess, meanwhile, found his Southern Pacific work dull and became careless in his work. He quit the job in the spring of 1891, and after securing a position as an instructor with the University of California, effective in the fall, he and Porter left the city for a two month trip for Europe.[167] Burgess spent the remainder of the summer with his mother and sisters in Boston and returned to San Francisco on September 1, the first day of classes. His new residence was at 1407 Jones Street, between Washington and Jackson. (We can see him inching gradually closer to a residence on Russian Hill.)

Over the next three years Burgess taught classes in mapping and technical drawing in the Civil Engineering and Drawing departments of the university. His duties must have left him a great deal of free time, for his other activities were numerous. Soon after his return in 1891 he established the Harrison Street Boys Club, for boys about twelve years of age who were largely from blue collar, South-of-Market families. It was modeled on clubs for underprivileged boys in New York and Boston and the settlement work of Jane Addams in Chicago. At first Burgess taught only a few

surveying land south and east of Los Angeles. At the completion of this job, in the spring of 1888, he moved to San Francisco to join his brother Howard and to continue working for SP in their offices. A romance dictated his move to Oakland that summer to be near Helen Hawes, daughter of an Episcopal minister. San Francisco also had its attractions — a Chinatown, a Latin Quarter, a dozen languages and more hills — and so it was back to the metropolis in 1890, to 1330 Washington Street, close to his ultimate Russian Hill haunts. He joined the Unitarian Church at Geary and Franklin streets, where he met and became friends with Bruce Porter.

Porter did not live on Russian Hill until the 1920s, and then only briefly, but he is a recurring figure in the history of the Summit and so deserves an introduction. He was born skills: hammock-weaving, woodcutting, and fret-sawing. He and his staff later added bookbinding, drawing, writing, typesetting, and printing. As the boys grew older they formed a debating team and studied military drill. Negative attitudes were expressed by the Boys Club toward saloons and cheap, juvenile fiction.

How the club was funded remains unknown, but it was an undeniable success. It won early praise and continued to operate long after Burgess left it and the city in 1897. Encouraged to continue in school beyond the ninth grade, some of the students went on to college to become professionals in art, music, architecture, law and even social work, following Burgess's example.

The accomplishment was remarkable for a young man of twenty-five (Burgess's age in 1891), but not everything went smoothly. Burgess still relished nonsense and had a strong sense of fun, and he tried to employ these traits to bolster his popularity with the students. Still, he was not all that popular. A New England conservatism and a superior attitude underlay his playful demeanor, and he lacked self-possession. Burgess was not as fun as he tried to be, Boys Club members remembered when they were interviewed many years later. "You had to take him as he was," said one, but some couldn't.[168]

Burgess also resumed his interest in the Unitarian Church after his return in from Europe. He published travel sketches and religious poetry in the church's Sunday school magazine and was active in its Onward Club. This group held an outing, Camp Ha-Ha, at a different northern California site each summer. Dressed like gypsies, in corduroys, denims, flannels, skirts and leggings, slouch hats and sombreros, the Unitarians arrived at the camp by stagecoach and on horseback bringing food, blankets, books and other diversions. Burgess added tobacco, candy, firecrackers, pen, paper

Florence Paul. *Courtesy Mrs. Arthur A. Moore.*

and ink; he later brought copies of *The Lark* to distribute. They stayed up late talking and singing beside a campfire, then slept in tents or beneath the stars.

Besides his teaching duties, the Boys Club, and the church, Burgess found time for almost daily visits to his neighbors, a few of whom he romanced. His favorite was Florence Lundborg, an artist who studied under Arthur Mathews and lived at 1308 Jones, only a block from Burgess. She, Burgess, and Bruce Porter embarked on visits to the Britton and Reys at the southeast corner of Union and Taylor, and to Kate Atkinson and the Pauls at 1032 Broadway. Burgess developed friendships with both of these families, often going directly from the Reys to the Paul household or vice-versa, staying for dinner, and sometimes not leaving until late at night. On Sundays he, Florence Lundborg, the Parkers (of 1601 Taylor), Kate Atkinson and the Pauls would walk to and from the Unitarian Church together, and there they met the Porters and Charles Murdock, who later printed *The Lark*.

He had a lukewarm and probably brief romance with Sylvia Rey in October, 1891, writing in his diary that once they "had a rather stupid time, as we generally do unless we have something special to do — I can't think of things." He had a friendship with Florrie Paul that was warmer and much longer lasting. Soon he met Annie Sheppard of the House of the Flag (southeast corner of Vallejo and Taylor) and began to date her as well.

Helen Hawes of Oakland, Florence Lundborg, Florence Paul, Sylvia Rey, Annie Sheppard — he saw them all in late 1891 and 1892. Often three or more of them were present on the same excursion. Sometimes the heartache was Frank's. After an "Enigma Party" thrown by Kate Atkinson he wrote in his diary, "Helen there I felt all [illegible] and was decidedly not at my best." After a cemetery walk with Florence, Florrie, and Charles B. Porter, Jr. (Bruce's brother) he wrote "At the last she [Florence Lundborg] told me we had been reputed engaged & we had better see less of each other." Later he had a rather exciting pillow fight with Miss Lundborg, but restrained himself from kissing her in close quarters, proving satisfactorily to her that he respected her. He later realized she had planned the exercise as a test.

For the most part, however, romance was subordinate to friendship in these relationships. Annie Sheppard, who had as many beaux as Burgess had girlfriends, later wrote, "He was the only young man who I was not afraid was going to fall in love with me. He was just an inspiring playmate."

From Burgess's diaries it is apparent that 1032 Broadway emerged as the primary gathering place for a large circle of friends. The occasions were dinners, parties, and drop-in visits; the guests were Burgess, the Porters, the Parkers, Florence Lundborg and her family, the Polks, Charles Murdock, Thomas and Mary Curtis Richardson, Porter Garnett, and occasional others. Almarin B. Paul and his daughters, Jane and Florrie, helped Kate Atkinson host the events. An artistic background, a Russian Hill (or nearby) address, and Unitarianism were the most common themes they had in common.

Kate Atkinson, dark haired, short, with dark brown eyes, aged forty-six in 1891, was the magnet that attracted and the glue that bound the group. Known to them as "Cudden Kate," because she and the Paul sisters were cousins, she organized the parties and captivated the guests with her sense of humor. Burgess's diary entries of 1892, sketchy as they are, are the only surviving evidence of their activities: On January 6th Miss Atkinson hosted a Twelfth Night Party. At another gathering a week later, Burgess noted, she was "funny and Flor got so worked up they had to stop her." After a dinner Mrs. Richardson gave on the 28th, Burgess wrote, "Miss Atk. very funny... a jolly time generally." Frank, Bruce Porter, Helen Hawes, and Kate sang songs together at the Enigma Party on February 13th; and on May 1st a Miss King played an instrument while an "awful funny" Kate and Almarin Paul sang before a large group. There was storytelling at the Atkinson house on May 10th, and after refreshments "the Polks came around and serenaded and played on banjos and violins, & I read [illegible] to Dan Polk's music."[169]

When it was all over Burgess looked back on these times nostalgically, and he wrote to Kate Atkinson:

> I long for someone to giggle with. 7 o'clock p. m. is the worst of it and I'd like to walk in without knocking and crowd in next to you — how we'd quarrel and joke and not know which made us better friends — you're all right Cudden Kate; there are no wrinkles in your soul.[170]

Living room, Atkinson-Paul residence. Designed by Willis Polk. From *The Home.*

Some significant changes were made to the Atkinson residence in the two years after the events described above. In the latter half of 1893 Atkinson hired Willis Polk to make changes to the first floor interior of her house. Polk put in classically detailed ceilings and wall paneling, a staircase with a classical arcade, and new cabinets, all of carved redwood. He also added two new fireplaces, one in the entrance hall with an exquisitely carved redwood mantle, and one of terra cotta in the living room. The feeling here is more sumptuous and elegant than were the rustic interiors of his Vallejo Street residences.[171]

During the Midwinter Fair of 1894 Atkinson employed Japanese gardeners from the Fair's tea garden to landscape the grounds of her house. The same year she traveled to Japan and brought back art objects to decorate the house with. Finally, when Broadway was graded in 1894, she placed a long classical balustrade along the retaining wall and installed a wrought iron entrance gate, both of which are still in place. There still remained in the 1890s many objects from earlier decades, including a Persian rug, a large oval table which had been shipped around the horn, and a piano with a copper front which had belonged to the Pauls in Nevada.[172]

*   *   *

In 1893 Frank Gelett Burgess moved from 1407 Jones Street to his first Russian Hill address, the Summerton Apartments at 1100 Green, where he lived with his brother Howard.[173] Not long afterward he pulled a stunt that changed the course of his life. On January 1, 1894 he and three friends mounted a successful assault on the infamous Cogswell statue on Market Street.

Dr. Henry D. Cogswell was a wealthy dentist and the benevolent founder of Cogswell

Atkinson house, carved wood column, arcade, and mantlepiece in entrance hall. From Willis Polk's 1893 remodeling. Photos by author.

College, a vocational school in the Mission District. As a teetotaler, he sought to lead others down the path of sobriety. His method was to erect statues of himself around the city, each mounted on a tall base and holding out a glass of pure Spring Valley tap water. Many found the statues offensive, none more so than the Bohemians of the city who considered them an affront to their lifestyle. The worst, all agreed, was the one near the foot of Market Street, almost the first sight to greet Midwinter Fair visitors as they disembarked from the ferry.

Two attempts to topple the statue had failed. Now Burgess, Bruce Porter, his brother Robert Porter, and John Harrold met at the statue late at night to try themselves. Burgess went to a store that he knew was open to buy some rope, and after the last California Street cable car had left they looped the rope around the statue and pulled it down with a heave.

The *Examiner* praised the stunt, calling the statue an "eyesore" which "dried up the artistic fountain of the soul." Basking in such praise, Burgess could not keep quiet, was identified, and was subsequently fired by the University of California. He then went to work for John Harrold's father, who custom made furniture and paid on a piecework basis. Although Burgess's income was modest and intermittent, the irregularity of the work suited him.[174]

Burgess' Bohemian lifestyle was now an accomplished fact. Although he had not left his job as an instructor voluntarily, he had arranged events so that no other outcome was possible. His next step, accomplished during the first half of 1894, was to move from his modern apartment building at Green and Leavenworth into a dilapidated old house on the Summit of Russian Hill, where he could pursue Bohemianism in a more appropriate setting.

His new home was 1031 Vallejo, a one story-plus-attic house at the southwest corner of Vallejo and Florence (the street his friend Florrie Paul had been named after). Built in the 1860s, it was one of fifteen small, unpretentious houses huddled together in the western third of the block between Florence and Jones streets. 1031 Vallejo was especially plain, for it lacked even the window moldings, overhanging cornice, or projecting eaves of its neighbors, and

Gelett Burgess residence, 1031 Vallejo, at Florence. California Historical Society.

its sides were merely blank walls. It was, however, a house all Burgess's own, it had a fine view of the Golden Gate, and it was close to the friends he had been visiting for three years. A nickname, "The Peanut Shell," was bestowed upon it, probably because short Mr. Burgess was sometimes called "The Walking Peanut."

The house had a dual function, as Burgess's residence and as the "Russian Hill Neighborhood House." There is no strong evidence as to what the Neighborhood House actually was. One possibility, that it was a sort of neighborhood meeting hall, similar to improvement club halls in other districts, seems unlikely. The other possibility that comes to mind is that it was a service organization for youth similar to the Harrison Street Boys Club. There was a need for such in the neighborhood. A *San Francisco Chronicle* article in 1889 identified seven hoodlum gangs in the city that year, one of which was located in the blocks bounded by Jackson, Broadway, Jones and Hyde streets, touching corners with the Summit. "Most of their wickedness," wrote the *Chronicle*, "finds vent in annoying women, robbing small children on their way to the groceries, stoning Chinese washhouses, and slogging belated citizens."[175]

This is speculative, but it is possible that residents of the neighborhood, aware of Burgess's marginal income, paid for the rent at 1031 Vallejo and actively recruited him to replicate his Harrison Street Boys Club on Russian Hill. Whatever its use, the Neighborhood House was formally organized in June, 1894 and lasted for three years. Kate Atkinson was the treasurer for at least part of this period, and workers besides Burgess included, at different times, Mary Curtis Richardson, Mary Gamble, Florence Paul, Mrs. W. B. Slocum (who lived at 1019 Vallejo with

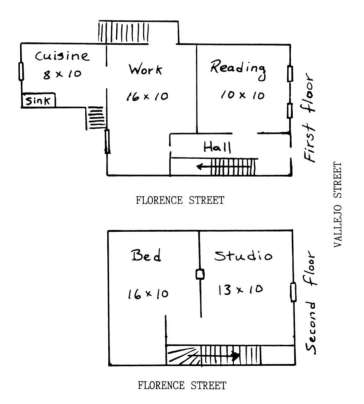

Plan of the Gelett Burgess residence, 1031 Vallejo Street, 1894. Redrawn from a plan by Gelett Burgess. Notebook #20, Gelett Burgess Papers, Bancroft Library.

Gelett Burgess at one of his Russian Hill residences. Gelett Burgess Collection, Bancroft Library.

Dora Williams), Bertha Wright (probably a Swedenborgian, as her relative Alice was), and several others, all women. The "membership" in 1896-1897 was seventy-nine, which perhaps meant the number of youths who attended classes there. Unfortunately, there are no descriptions of the Neighborhood House's activities.[176]

As for the house itself, there was "no queerer, quainter, crookeder a house, nor a house in worse array, of more tatterdemalion an aspect and cock-sided disrepute than the chunk of queer cottage at No. 1031 Vallejo Street," as Burgess himself wrote in one of his novels.[177] Inside, Japanese prints covered his cracked plaster walls, and oddities that Burgess had collected or created could be found on mantlepiece and table. One such was a bust of Abraham Lincoln which, according to Burgess, contemplated "the inconsistencies of modern manners." A sign at its base reading "I Wonder

Why!" revealed to the observer what the emancipator was thinking.

Lacking regular work, the Walking Peanut would appear at mid-morning on his rear porch clad in a red flannel bath robe, "addressing a scrap of broken mirror" as he shaved. For a time he would sit at the north window of his attic story and alternate between gazing at the view and writing busily. Next it was off to the "Lower Town" — North Beach, Chinatown, and the retail district on Kearny Street — which Burgess reached by descending the goat path along Vallejo to Taylor. On Kearny he bought California violets for the ladies and a large carnation to put in his lapel, either in burlesque or fond imitation of Oscar Wilde. He lunched variously on frijoles at Luna's, on upper Dupont (10 cents), or on filet of sole at Campi's, on Clay Street (12 1/2 cents).

Evenings might find him entertaining at home. He had a pink couch which, he wrote, would "hold say six, but if the men and maids you mix 'twill hold an equal number more, the rest can sit upon the floor." For entertainment he promised "something modest, an opera, maybe, would be oddest." On one occasion he promised his guests a distinguished visitor from New York; it turned out to be a mannequin of clothes stuffed with rags. On another he set up a large crucifix backlit by candles which cast its shadow eerily across a wall, creating a "satisfactorily unholy" atmosphere.

"I guess we were all heathens then," Annie Sheppard said later.[178]

Jokes became his métier. He once "mailed" a letter by dropping it out of the second story window of a friend's house, just to see if it would reach its destination. (It did.) At a dinner gathering he was sent upstairs to fetch some fruit, and he rolled the fruit down the stairs ahead of him, declaring it would not wait for him, and he could not keep up. At the residences of his girlfriends' parents' he would collapse on a couch and splay his feet out, refusing to be self-contained, and embarrassing his girls.

Such behavior wore on his friends, but Burgess refused to be contrite. In 1897, while admitting that he "kept his friends busy with apologies for his rudeness and conceit," he also bragged that he had "pulled down public statues."[179] In one of his nonsense poems for *The Lark* he was probably describing himself when he wrote

I love to go to Lectures'
And make the Audience stare,
By walking round upon their heads
And spoiling People's hair![180]

At least one person was wild enough to enjoy this side of him. Elsie Martinez, widow of artist Xavier Martinez, remembered him in 1969: "A little short fellow, he had plenty of personality and a most amazing voice. He used to sing cowboy and French revolutionary songs, bellowing like a bull. You could hear him a block away. He loved jokes."[181]

It is tempting to compare Burgess's brashness with Willis Polk's. Both men were very short, and they may have developed their egos as compensation. The resemblance ends there, however. Polk simply did not care much what people thought of him, and was often disrespectful of others. Burgess's rudeness was not of that sort. He liked people very much, and wanted their affection in return. He resorted to odd and often unsuccessful methods of attaining this end.

*   *   *

Gelett Burgess and Bruce Porter made a new friend in 1895, courtesy of Dora Williams, an artist of an older generation. In May of that year, Fanny Van de Grift Stevenson, the widow of Robert Louis Stevenson, came to live at 1019 Vallejo.

This must have been electrifying to Burgess and Porter, for if they had a literary idol, it was "RLS." Porter still affected a Stevensonian appearance, wearing a black flowing tie every day, and Burgess, well-read as he was, once considered Stevenson the one "great man in the world."[182] The two were greatly saddened when Stevenson died in December, 1894.

That his widow came to live with Dora Williams was not surprising, for the two women had long been close friends. They shared in common two traits which meant everything: style and attitude. Both were extremely liberated for their time. Dora was a "slim, straight-backed, decisive Yankee woman who prided herself on a frankness that was sometimes," according to Fanny's biographer, "rather appalling." Her attire of "unbecoming hats," silks, velvets, necklaces, and many items (such as a silver mesh purse, pencil case, and penknife) which hung by chains from her belt was similarly assertive.[183] Fanny smoked. Dora had married a divorced artist; Fanny had divorced to marry a sickly, possible dying, writer who had come from England to be with her. It was Dora Williams who had urged Fanny and RLS to marry in 1880, soon after Fanny's divorce, instead of waiting a year in seemly fashion, and it was Dora who convinced Dr. Samuel Merritt of Oakland to rent the Stevensons his yacht, the *Casco*, for a trip to the Marquesas in 1888.

After Robert Louis Stevenson's death in Samoa, Fanny, her son Lloyd, and her daughter Belle moved to San Francisco to live in Dora Williams' house, where they remained for half of 1895.[184] Burgess and Porter were quickly invited into friendship with Mrs. Stevenson. Fanny and Dora, Frank and Bruce became a foursome, and their favorite activity was attending seances at the homes of "mediums" in the Uptown Tenderloin. They took the revelations with some seriousness. Once Dora claimed to receive a message from RLS, and Fanny, herself susceptible to such matters, chided her friend for her gullibility at lights and sounds made in dark rooms. The two quarreled, and made up.[185] Such dabbling in the supernatural may have spread to other residents of the Summit at this time, for Kate Atkinson was also said to have held seances at her house.[186]

Although he was twenty-six years her junior, Gelett Burgess and Fanny Stevenson began a romance at this time. It did not last long, for the Stevensons left San Francisco for Hawaii in November, 1895. Nevertheless, Burgess designed RLS's tomb in 1896, and the romance was resumed with considerable passion in 1898 when Burgess and Fanny were both in England.

Fanny Stevenson's arrival at 1019 Vallejo in May, 1895 coincided with the first issue of *The Lark*, Burgess and Porter's contribution to artistic expression at the *fin de siecle*. In a sense they were part of a trend, for little magazines flourished in America with the rise of the Arts and Crafts movement, the Art Nouveau style, and Oscar Wildeian decadence. Burgess had his own ideas about what an artistic magazine should be, and after five years in San Francisco in company with talented friends, he was ready to put his ideas into material form.

*   *   *

For some time Burgess had been writing humorous nonsense verse and making unusual drawings for his own and others' amusement. He would leave such verse at the doors of the women he knew in lieu of the usual love poems. Two children that he knew were also recipients of his efforts. They were Arnold and Robin Weber, sons of Margaret Weber, Bruce Porter's sister. Burgess became a sort of adopted uncle to them, and he made three booklets of verse and colored drawings for them in 1894. Much of this material was adapted for *The Lark* the following year.[187]

Burgess and Porter were more or less equal partners in *The Lark* at its beginning. Besides their shared admiration for the spirit of Stevenson, they wanted to publish lighthearted material to represent the "new California." They disliked the sophisticated decadence of recent little magazines such as *The Yellow Book* and *The Chap Book*, and intended their own magazine as a foil to such negativity. Burgess put it this way:

> We do not care for satire, parody, local color, "timeliness," or black pessimism; what we wish is something inspired with a true joie de vivre, something that would be comprehensible as well to your grandchildren as to your grandfather and yourself.[188]

Porter wrote:

> We demolished Decadence and picked Hope out of the dust-heap, and with a fine enthusiasm took her to lunch with us at the *Restaurant aux Gourmets* [where] the LARK was named in a baptism of *vin ordinaire*....[189]

The first issue appeared in May, 1895. Measuring 5 1/2" by 7 1/2", sixteen pages in length, the most remarkable feature about it physically was the paper it was printed on. As an economy measure the editors had searched through Chinatown until they found a textured paper made of bamboo fiber which had been shipped from China in bales, and stamped on the ends with red and green Chinese characters. Another cost-saver was the lack of justified right-hand margins. These features, and the ragged edges, added artistic flair to the magazine.

Charles Murdock was the printer, and briefly, at first, the publisher. His press at 532 Clay was appropriately located across the street from a Bohemian hangout, Campi's restaurant; and the press room, situated above a produce and poultry market, was reached by a steep, narrow stairway. The role of publisher quickly passed from Murdock to William Doxey, who owned a bookstore in the Palace Hotel. He hired Fanny Stevenson's daughter Isobel Strong as a clerk, and as *The Lark* gained fame he hung a sign outside his shop which read "At the Sign of The Lark."

The Lark soon gained a wide readership. One of Burgess's nonsense pieces from the first issue, "The Purple Cow," was quickly reprinted nationally, and it became the most famous thing he ever did.[190] There was a Stevenson tribute by Porter in the second issue, and the third featured Burgess's "Peculiar History of the Chewing-Gum Man," forty-six rhymed couplets about a creature "a-most as high as the Palace Hotel" created by children who spent a year chewing gum. ("The Purple Cow" was taken from a booklet Burgess made for the Weber boys, and "Chewing-Gum Man" was from a gift he made for Kate Atkinson in November, 1894.)

Porter soon lost interest in this sort of flighty material, and Burgess had to produce the third issue by himself. Although Porter appeared frequently thereafter, he later explained, "I am sorry to confess that my contributions were written off hand and in street cars or in restaurants — when Burgess made a demand."[191] *The Lark* was now Burgess's to nurture.

He began to solicit contributions. Florence Lundborg, Ernest Peixotto, and Porter Garnett were by far the most frequent new contributors, and the first two designed most of the covers. (Both Lundborg and Garnett were working as teachers at the Harrison Street Boys Club, as was Peixotto's sister.) They, Porter and Burgess began calling themselves *Les Jeunes* — the young ones — and they worked together in general harmony. Other artists and writers were also recruited. The most popular was a young Japanese poet, Yone Noguchi, who lived with Joaquin Miller at the "Hights" in Oakland for several years and went on to international recognition. Juliet Wilbor Tompkins, Carolyn Wells, and Willis Polk contributed a few items each, and Maynard Dixon, one.[192] Evocative dream-poems, essays, obscure short stories, Burgess's illustrated nonsense verse, and impressionistic cover drawings is probably as good a way as any of characterizing the material. In short, *The Lark* defied generalizations, except that it was unconventional. There were enough surprises to keep readers interested for two years.

The magazine became so popular that Doxey began to publish spin-off products, usually posters taken from the covers by Lundborg. The magazine's print run gradually increased from 3,000 to 5,000, the price

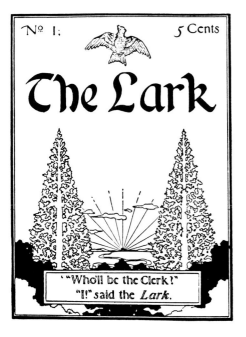

The Lark: cover of the first issue, May, 1895.

"The Purple Cow," from the first issue of *The Lark,* May, 1895.

doubling to ten cents. Toward the end the publisher Doxey was able to pay editor Burgess a salary of seventy-five dollars a month.

After twenty-four issues, however, everyone (except Doxey, who was making a profit) agreed that enough was enough. The last regular issue was published in April, 1897, and the commemorative, farewell number, the *Epi-Lark,* was issued in May. The *Chap-Book* summed up the feeling: "Even the sincerest friends of the paper are glad, for a constant atmosphere of nonsense-rhyme was growing almost as debilitating to the reader as it must have been to the writer." The Chicago *Evening Post* conjectured, more critically, that Burgess and Porter had worked with the "incense of slowly burning joss-sticks in the air." Ambrose Bierce had this to say of *The Lark* in *The Wasp*: "That it did not expire more prematurely is entirely due to the ignorance of the community that it ever existed."[193] But anyone could have predicted that *The Lark* would not have been Bierce's cup of tea.

Burgess, through *The Lark,* helped create the impression nationally that California was

a little different from the rest of the country. A few, at least, saw the state as a place of unreality, of romanticism, rather than hard realism. Californians tended to be lotus-eaters and dreamers, and as a result, thought Edmund Wilson, their literature would never carry a "weight proportionate to the bulk of their work."[194]

This would be especially true of Burgess. Though he ultimately wrote over thirty books, including many novels, only a few made a mark, and he never approached the great career that many predicted for him.[195]

Shortly before the demise of *The Lark* Frank Norris quit his post of editorial assistant at *The Wave,* and editor John O'Hara Cosgrove hired Burgess as a replacement. (Until this time Burgess had continued to work as a designer of furniture for Harrold, Belcher and Allen.) For two months Burgess interviewed actresses and otherwise covered theater activity in San Francisco for *The Wave.* It was a "real job," as we would say today, but this material is far less memorable than what Burgess did for *The Lark.* The ephemeral nature of such journalism may have weighed on Burgess's mind, for he declared in *The Wave* that "I have gone a-larking, and made some talk perhaps, but I intend to work seriously hereafter."

He seemed a little confused about how to do so. With the *Epi-Lark* out, Burgess quit his job at *The Wave*; and on May 17th he left 1031 Vallejo, Russian Hill and San Francisco for the publishing centers on the east coast. In New York he visited with the luminaries, William Dean Howells, John Kendrick Bangs, and others. He filled letters home and the newspapers with accounts of his exploits, so that others grew envious and followed him. Frank Norris, who considered his work much more serious than Burgess's, went "ash grey" when Porter read him one such letter, and beat a table with clenched fists, exclaiming, "Damn him! Damn him! He's got it and it belongs to me!"[196] Norris and Peixotto went to New York, Porter and Lundborg to Europe. They need not have worried about being eclipsed by Burgess, however.

He tried stringing together his series of Vivette Papers from *The Lark* into a novel, *Vivette*. Two 1897 editions brought Burgess $300, but reviews were not uniformly favorable. ("More cleverness has been wasted on it than one finds in a dozen ordinary books," read one.)[197] He also wrote about thirty stories, essays, reviews, and nonsense pieces that year, selling eleven. Considering that *Vivette* was recycled material, it was not much of a showing.

There followed a trip to Europe, where he resumed his romance with Fanny Stevenson. In 1900 he returned to San Francisco, where he lived in two residences on the West Slope of Russian Hill.[198] He settled down to work then, collaborating with Russian Hill resident Will Irwin on two novels set locally, *The Reign of Queen Isyl* (1903) and *The Picaroons* (1904).[199]

The former of these appears to have sold quite well. Then it was to New York again, where he responded to the destruction of San Francisco in 1906 by writing *The Heart Line*, an exceptionally readable romance of the old city.

The rest of his life was eventful, if not very happy. He published many books (mysteries, romances, tongue-in-cheek self-improvement, and eight Goops books for children) knew such people as Franklin D. Roosevelt, Henry James, and Picasso, and split his time between New York and Paris. He was often in the news, often broke, and burdened with an unhappy marriage. At the end of his life he moved to Carmel to care for his sister, and on the way he paid a final visit to the Summit, a half century after his *Les Jeunes* days. The "Peanut Shell" was long gone, but the Atkinson, Polk, and Williams residences still stood. He died in Carmel in 1951.

What shall we make of Gelett Burgess? Do the flaws in his personality and the slightness of his writing relegate him to the status of a minor figure? Why have so many people continued writing about him, even to recent years?

The best thing about Burgess is that his sense of fun and love of nonsense, observable from an early age, were inherent in his nature. The delight he took in *The Lark*, his Goops, and San Francisco were genuine, and this comes through in his work. Early success seems to have gone to his head, however. It inhibited his growth as a writer, and he could not recognize when his audience had had enough of a certain kind of joke. (He attempted to have a Broadway musical made of "The Purple Cow" as late as the 1920s.) In his early work, though, the genuineness shows. Much of it still delights us, and always will, but we also find ourselves wishing that he had done a little better.

Horatio P. Livermore. Courtesy George Livermore.

Half a year after Gelett Burgess departed the Summit, Horatio P. and Helen Eels Livermore arrived. The move was not entirely by choice. The family had suffered financial reverses and were forced to sell their Rockridge Park mansion along with its spacious grounds.[200] Horatio still owned the house at 1023 Vallejo on Russian Hill which he had rented to Willis Polk in 1891-1892, and it now became their new home. For the Livermores, this two story house on a 50-vara lot definitely qualified as reduced circumstances.

According to an often-repeated story, Mrs. Livermore had been invited to one of Polk's parties at this house, and she so admired his remodeling in redwood that she evicted him so the Livermores could move in.[201] This story cannot be true, for an interim tenant, Frank F. Stone, rented 1023 Vallejo from the Livermores during 1893-1897. Stone moved across the street to 1036 Vallejo when the Livermores needed 1023 for their own occupancy.[202] Thus began a century of Livermore residency on the Summit of Russian Hill.

Horatio P. Livermore was an industrialist on a grand scale, and like many industrialists who break new ground, he found development expenses to be overwhelming. Much of his work, were it to be undertaken today, would certainly be opposed by environmentalists, but in his own time projects such as Livermore's were by consensus considered vital to the needs of an expanding population.

The first Livermore in America came from England in 1634, and in 1779 Elijah Livermore founded the town of Livermore, Maine. In 1850 Elijah's grandson, Horatio Gates Livermore, traveled overland from Independence, Missouri, to California.[203] Already familiar with the lumber and water power industries, he hoped at an early date to develop an industrial city on the American River that would be based on logging and water-powered sawmills. The realization of such dreams would consume his entire life, and would reach fruition only after his death.

His sons, Horatio and Charles, followed him west in 1856. Horatio Putnam Livermore did not at first join his father on the American River, but went to work in San Francisco for the west coast branch of Redington and Co., a wholesale drug firm he had worked for in Boston. By the 1860s he was a partner in the firm and the treasurer of Redington's quicksilver company in Lake County.

Meanwhile, on the American River in

1862, Horatio Gates Livermore gained control of the Natoma Water and Mining Co. for the purpose of acquiring its water rights. He also purchased a large tract of land that had been part of William Leidesdorff's Rancho de los Americanos. He planted orchards and vineyards and built a fruit drying plant and winery at Folsom.

Water power remained his real goal, and the elder Livermore began construction of the first Folsom Dam in 1867. Delays consumed many years, but the dam project moved forward again in the late 1880s when, in exchange for the use of convict labor, the Livermores transferred land to the state for a penitentiary.

By this time Horatio P. Livermore had joined his father in the enterprise, and under his guidance its nature began to evolve. The use of flowing water as a direct motive force was being supplanted by hydro-electric power, and Horatio Putnam knew that the dam would be obsolete by the time it was completed unless it was adapted to that purpose. To create a market for the dam's projected hydroelectric power, Livermore obtained an electric street railway franchise and founded a power company in Sacramento, twenty-two miles away. Through a long series of transcontinental negotiations, he was able to get financing from the newly formed General Electric Company for the construction of a power house and transmission lines. Horatio Gates Livermore, who died early in 1892, did not live to see the completion of the dam and the generation of electric power the following year. For Horatio Putnam Livermore, the triumph was muted by competition from other power companies and by political opposition which blocked the sale of his electrical power. Cash flow became even more of a problem during the winter of 1897-1898 when a major drought reduced hydroelectric activity. With revenues low, General Electric began to assume more and

more control of Livermore's company, the Sacramento Electric, Gas and Railway Co., to protect their investment.

Another drain on Livermore's finances was his American River and Land Company, which he commenced in 1889 with the purchase of 9,000 acres of timberland located between the south and middle forks of the American River. A forty mile logging road was built, and the river was cleared of boulders so that logs could be floated downstream to a new sawmill. When operations commenced in 1897, however, it was discovered that rock shelves and other obstructions prevented the logs from reaching their destination in good condition. Although much logging was done, it had to be discontinued after a few years.[204]

Such were the problems that drained Horatio P. Livermore's finances and led his family to move to 1023 Vallejo Street at the end of 1897. The family then consisted of Horatio, age sixty; his second wife Helen Eels, thirty-nine; Horatio's adult children by his first wife, Edith, Norman, and Mattie; and Horatio and Helen's daughter, Elizabeth. They had a servant of long standing, Lim Ti Ark, a native of China

Lim Ti Ark. He was the Livermore family servant for eighty years. Courtesy George Livermore.

The Livermore Meadow. Immediately north of the Livermore residence these brick steps led to a broad grassy area, the "Meadow." Today, the Meadow is an excavated pit awaiting development. Courtesy George Livermore.

who had worked for and lived with the Livermores since about 1870, when he was seventeen. Ark would remain with the family until his death in 1950 at age ninety-seven.[205]

It appears that Horatio was not overjoyed with the prospect of living on Russian Hill, whereas Helen, who had more artistic sensibilities, felt attracted to the neighborhood and its shingled architecture. An added attraction for them both was the presence of Worcester, who had tutored the children many years earlier when he lived in Piedmont. A desire to be close to him may well have determined the Livermores' choice of residence after selling their Rockridge Park estate.[206]

The Livermores made some alterations to their house about the time they moved in. A two story addition was built on the west end,

facing Florence Street, and an extension to the second story was made on the east, overhanging the main entrance. Classical columns were placed under the overhang to support the second story, and the entire structure was coated with brown shingles. The result was a larger house, but one ungainly in appearance. The only element of David M. Morrison's 1854 house left intact after this work was the slightly pitched roofline.[207]

The orchard planted many years earlier by George R. Turner still grew in the yard facing Vallejo Street, and now a tea house was built near the northwest corner of the lot. Brick pathways led through the yard from Vallejo Street to the residence and tea house. As the path approached the residence, the elevation dropped, and the path became eleven brick

Ethel Parker and Edith Livermore, ca. 1900. Nurse Ethel, who lived nearby at 1601 Taylor, comforts Edith, who was badly injured in a riding accident. Courtesy George Livermore.

steps leading down to the house. The upper portion of the yard, that closer to Vallejo Street, was always referred to by the Livermores as "the Meadow."

H. P. Livermore's power company began to show profits at the turn of the century, but in March, 1903, when Horatio was sixty-five, he and his investment partners sold the Sacramento Electric, Gas, and Railway Company to an aggressive new power company, the California Gas and Electric Corporation. This company was founded by Eugene de Sabla and John Martin as a consolidation of their several smaller companies, and successive mergers over the next two years led to the creation of the Pacific Gas and Electric Company (P. G. and E.) in 1905. Horatio Livermore's Folsom Dam and hydroelectric power house were considered an important element of the fledgling, giant power

company. As for Livermore himself, after decades of struggle in this arena, he had had enough.[208]

Photo albums compiled by his daughter Edith record something of the family life on Russian Hill at the time of Horatio's retirement. Edith, then thirty-three, had been seriously injured in a riding accident not long before, leaving her a semi-invalid for life. In one photograph, she is sitting on the steps to the Meadow with her neighbor Ethel Parker, of 1601 Taylor. Ethel, granddaughter of Charles and Maria Homer, appears to be playing the comforting nurse to injured Edith. Soon afterward, in about 1904, Edith and Mattie left to pursue literary and artistic lives in Europe: Edith to Berlin, and Mattie to London, where she would marry a music teacher. Edith returned to San Francisco many years later, residing in houses on Florence Street that her brother Norman had built.

Norman was just settling into his career. He had attended Cornell University and graduated in 1895 as a civil engineer. He worked in the east for awhile, then returned to help his father in the hydroelectric industry prior to the sale of Horatio's company to de Sabla and Martin. Now, in 1905, Norman formed his own company, which sold railway, logging, mining, concrete, and other heavy construction machinery.[209]

Horatio was now retired, but could not remain idle. He dabbled in various business investments and maintained, with Norman, an office in the splendid new Rialto Building at New Montgomery and Mission. Still, his time was freer now, and he turned his attention to the family home on Russian Hill.

He had never completely reconciled himself to living there. He liked the idea of moving to Santa Barbara, and floated the idea every now and then to Helen. She, however, wanted to stay on the Summit. Horatio, accordingly, began to make long term plans for

The Livermore house, 1906. This view is looking north from Nob Hill toward Russian Hill. Courtesy George Livermore.

the enlargement of their house and the further development and beautification of the neighborhood.

In June, 1903, three months after the sale of the power company became final, Horatio hired a neighbor, architect Edward L. Holmes, to make further additions to 1023 Vallejo.[210] A third story with a double-pitch hipped roof was added, and projecting additions supported by classical columns were built onto the north and south sides of the house. The house, still coated with brown shingles, was now rimmed on three sides by columns. The effect was unified and well-proportioned, a decided improvement over the additions of 1897-1898. As for David Morrison's one story house of 1854, it was now all but buried within the second story.

Horatio next turned his attention to the neighborhood. One of the drawbacks that Horatio felt needed correcting was the collection of small 1850s and 1860s houses on the west side of Florence Street, opposite his house. It appears that he felt finer residences should eventually be built there. He and Norman did buy one of the houses, 9 Florence (where #39 is today) and planned to build a stable there for the family's use. The Livermores may have been thinking of buying other lots for development purposes as 1906 approached.

Horatio also took upon himself the improvement of the Vallejo Street access to the Summit. As early as 1894 Willis Polk had written, "With the goat path up Vallejo Street properly converted into a series of terraces, and these lots properly improved, there could be no prettier place in San Francisco." Quite possibly Polk and Livermore had discussed collaborating on such improvements before the turn of the century.

Now, upon his retirement, Horatio canvassed the neighborhood for funds and retained Polk, now back from working for Burnham in Chicago, to design a terraced concrete stairway along the Vallejo Street right-of-way, from Taylor west to the top of the hill. There would also be matching improvements at Vallejo and Jones which would replace an old wooden stairway that Horatio had often "anathematized." The neighbors negotiated with Gray Brothers, concrete contractors, to do the work, and it appears that the project was close to commencement when the earthquake and fire of 1906 resulted in its postponement for eight long years.[211]

In mid-April all of the Livermores were out of town except for Horatio. Helen, Elizabeth, and Lim Ti Ark were vacationing in Santa Barbara; Norman was in Seattle on business; and Edith and Mattie were in Europe. Horatio had the house to himself. Norman returned to San Francisco on the 16th of the month, in time to experience the city's great earthquake. Both he and Horatio would play major roles in the effort to save the Summit from burning in the subsequent fire.

Helen Eels Livermore at home, 1904. This shows the interior as remodeled by Willis Polk in 1891. Courtesy George Livermore.

Troubled Times at the "House of Many Corners"

After Samuel Theller's long occupancy of the old Ranlett house — then numbered 1607 Taylor, now 1637 — the house went through eight years of mostly absentee ownership. The several owners during this period (1886-1894) appear to have viewed the property mainly for its income potential, and so, not surprisingly, the 50-vara lot was partitioned. Dora Williams' and Willis Webb Polk's lots were carved out of it in 1892, and a parcel at the corner of Vallejo and Taylor was sold off as well. When the house was sold again, in August, 1894, it occupied a sixty-five foot lot — only a few feet wider than the house itself. The buyers of the house and its reduced lot were Everard M. and Margaretta Morgan, and as a result of their unfortunate three year ownership William H. Ranlett's "House of Many Corners" would never be the same again.

Everard Milton Morgan was a man with a past. As a lawyer and notary public, he had not only dabbled in Fresno County politics and enjoyed political patronage, he had engaged in forgeries and abused his position as a notary to embezzle thousands of dollars. After he fled to Honolulu to escape prosecution, his wife Margaretta spent considerably of her own inherited estate to clear his name and allow him to return to California. The Morgans moved to San Francisco in 1890 and Everard promptly returned to his old ways. Dressing in shabby clothes, and creating the impression by his appearance that he cared little for the fine things in life, he earned a wide reputation as an energetic and successful collector of hopeless old debts. He "never let up," it was said, and when he collected, his grateful clients, mostly doctors and dentists, nearly always agreed to allow him to invest the proceeds for them. By paying out small amounts of interest now and then, he managed to avoid a settling of accounts and to stave off prosecution. He was also retained by women who needed quick divorces, and he was always able to secure the documents they wanted, although upon investigation the documents proved not to be genuine. During the six years after his return Morgan actively defrauded dozens of clients (most for only $70 to $100, and a few for up to $4,000) without once landing in serious trouble. Meanwhile Margaretta, to whom he had been married since 1877, and whose inheritance he had spent, continued to look on indulgently.[212]

Morgan's biggest victim by far was a wealthy Sacramento realtor of genial disposition and general popularity named Edwin K. Alsip. Alsip had a branch office in San Francisco's Mills Building and was often in the city on business... and more than business. He sometimes attended a church in the Mission district, and there, according to one version of the story, he became enamoured of an attractive single woman in her twenties, Eugenie Flora Howell, who had recently arrived from an eastern college and served the church as an organist. Although he was married, had four daughters, and was twice her age, he and Howell became lovers, and thus Edwin Alsip became vulnerable. When after some months Miss Howell feared she was pregnant, she consulted a physician named Nelson Giberson at his 121 Powell Street office. It so happened that Dr. Giberson was a friend of Everard Morgan, and together the two men conspired to blackmail Alsip.

For the scheme to work, Miss Howell's cooperation was needed, and it was obtained though a masterful use of psychology. Try to imagine the position of a single woman, far from home, believing herself pregnant by a married man, in nineteenth century America. Howell appears to have been terrified, and when Giberson and Morgan, posing as her friends, offered her a free room at the Morgan residence, 1607 Taylor, she accepted gladly. When Howell turned out not to be pregnant after all, the conspirators, by careful argument, convinced her that she had been ruthlessly wronged by Alsip, that he should pay, and that she should go along with their ruse. She agreed to do so. After several months had passed, Dr. Giberson was able to obtain a newborn foundling baby from the City and County Hospital. Since Alsip had only daughters, and since he had expressed interest to Howell in passing on the family name, a newborn male was selected. At the end of November, 1894 Alsip was invited to 1607 Taylor to visit his lover and "son," and at this time Morgan gently outlined to Alsip the benefits which he could derive by making monthly payments, as opposed to the costs of public exposure.[213]

For two years Alsip was expertly drained by Morgan. By one account, Alsip readily agreed to pay $4,000, most of which he believed would go to Miss Howell, whom he believed he had wronged; and he also agreed to pay another $60 per month for support of the child, which he would adopt in eleven years. This money having come so easily, Morgan felt emboldened to adopt a sterner demeanor and to demand more for his silence. Alsip subsequently paid over notes of up to $3,000, these coming due some years hence, again for the care of the baby. Instead of holding onto these notes, as he was supposed to do, Morgan sold them at a discount for immediate cash. In the end, the amount that Alsip paid was estimated at over $12,000.

Howell was sent back east with less than $400 for her trouble, and Morgan and Giberson split the rest of the money. The baby, unbeknownst to Alsip, was sent to Masonic Avenue to be cared for by Morgan's cousin, who had trouble collecting the twenty dollars monthly that she was promised for the infant's care. Occasionally Everard's brother, Bill Morgan, would drop by to take photos of little

Eugene, for forwarding to Alsip. For each photo he tried to pose the infant so that it resembled the supposed father.

In July, 1895, Margaretta Morgan finally lost patience with Everard and divorced him on grounds of infidelity. On paper she received a somewhat favorable settlement, for in addition to seventy-five dollars monthly alimony and custody of their three children, Everard deeded 1607 Taylor to her in September, 1895.[214] The house was mortgaged for $5,000, but he promised to pay it off. Margaretta continued living on the Summit, while Morgan moved to an apartment at 406 Sutter. He remarried in either December, 1895 or March, 1896 and moved with his new bride, Miss May Cramer of Benicia, to Broadway in Pacific Heights.

Everard Morgan never did make any mortgage payments on 1607 Taylor, and when she was about to loose the house, Margaretta filed suit. She also talked to Edwin Alsip a year after her divorce. Feeling sorry for him, she said, she went to Alsip in August, 1896 and explained how he had been duped. Alsip, however, had become devoted to the child he was convinced he had fathered, and refused to believe her. (By Alsip's version, it was a lawyer who first came to him with the truth. Alsip said he then interviewed Margaretta, who confirmed it.)

Alsip now felt less compliant when another demand for money came from Everard Morgan. This time he had no way of raising cash easily, and decided to hire investigators to look into Margaretta's (or the lawyer's) story. By December he had the facts, and he then confronted Morgan. He demanded the return of the notes, which Morgan no longer had, having sold them at discount. With some difficulty, Morgan raised the money to buy them back, but as a result he became squeezed by his other creditors. He also faced the lawsuit by Margaretta. Trapped at last, he fled San

Clockwise from top: Everard Milton Morgan, Edwin K. Alsip, "Eugene Jorgenson," and "Eugenie Flora Howell." Drawings from newspapers.

Francisco in March, 1897, only a day or two before his new wife gave birth.

Curiously, some of his creditors, impressed by Morgan's industriousness, believed that he could work things out if he was only allowed a little time, and they blamed Margaretta for her aggressive claims against him. After she recovered from giving birth Morgan's new wife joined in the chorus of blame against Margaretta; and while she was unsure of Everard's whereabouts, she told reporters she was sure he would return and make good if everyone would stop hounding him. As for Margaretta, she explained that she still wished her husband no ill will, and would like to see him reform.

Margaretta's critics were silenced when, a few days later, the story of Alsip, Flora Howell, and baby Eugene came out in the newspapers. Everard Morgan was soon found hiding in the redwoods and building a cabin about thirty miles north of Ukiah. He was arrested and returned to San Francisco.

The Morgan episode appears to have had an unfortunate effect upon the physical structure of 1607 Taylor. Sometime during the 1890s the house was cut in two, the southern portion remaining in place on Russian Hill and the northern portion being removed. Sanborn insurance maps prove that this happened between 1891 and 1899. According to oral history sources, the house was split as a divorce settlement, with the husband getting half the house, and the wife the other half.[215] There were other owners during the nineties besides the Morgans, but it seems certain the house was diminished under their calamitous stewardship. If so, Everard Morgan must have salvaged half of the structure under the terms of his settlement with Margaretta, then either selling it to a house mover or moving it himself in 1895.[216]

1607 Taylor, then, was a world apart from its neighbors on the Summit during the mid-

1890s. While Worcester, the Polks, Atkinson, the Pauls, the Richardsons, Gelett Burgess and Dora Williams entertained their friends and each other in neighborly warmth and good fellowship, Everard Morgan blackmailed and defrauded. There had been instances of financial disaster and family estrangement often enough in the Summit's history, but these sad events had been due more to common human frailties than actual malevolence. Morgan's predecessor at 1607 Taylor, Samuel Theller, had probably had an illegal role in the artificial inflation of San Miguel Rancho land prices for sale to homestead associations, but at least it can be said that no one was forced to buy the land. To Everard Morgan and his associates belongs the distinction of striking the most clearly sordid note in the Summit's known, 19th century history.

Margaretta Morgan did not long enjoy what remained of 1607 Taylor. The California Title Insurance and Trust Company, holder of the mortgage on the property, sued to foreclose on June 1, 1897, and after the required waiting period and auction they, the high bidders, took ownership on the last day of 1897.[217]

California Title further subdivided the lot. The northern portion, now vacant, was eventually sold to Robert Hanford, who built the conservatory of 1001 Vallejo there in 1905-1906. The back yard of 1607 Taylor was purchased by Norman Livermore, and years later it became the site of his step-mother's new Julia Morgan-designed home. As for the House of Fewer Corners, it now sat on a lot that varied from thirty-two to thirty-five feet wide by one hundred feet deep. The lot was just large enough to accommodate the house itself and a small back yard. Poor Ranlett, had he lived, would have been saddened at this violation of his suburban design ideals.

The next owner of the house also had a "past." For two years, 1899-1901, the house was home to D'Arcy and Kate Cashin. D'Arcy

Cashin had first worked in San Francisco in 1875 as a post office clerk, and he steadily rose in the ranks of the city's public servants. In rather quick succession he became the deputy Superintendent of Streets, a Custom House examiner, and the City and County Recorder. After a brief spell in private business, he was back at the Custom House in 1890 as the deputy Collector, where he may have found temptation too great to resist. In 1892 he was charged with defrauding the government on behalf of Liebes Bros., the tobacco importers, and Neuberger, Reis, and Co., dry goods merchants. It was Cashin who, in "99 cases out of a hundred," selected which cases of imported goods would go to the Appraiser's office to be appraised for taxation. Somehow only the filler tobacco went to the Appraiser, while more valuable wrapper tobacco went directly to Liebes; likewise, only cotton goods went to the Appraiser, while the "silks and satins" went to Neuberger, Reis and Co.'s warehouse without being inspected.

Cashin was dismissed by Collector Phelps, and he fled to British Columbia. Neuberger, Reis and Co. paid $106,000 to the government to escape prosecution. A year later Kate Cashin returned to San Francisco to plea for a reduction in her husband's bail so that he could stand trial. At length this was arranged, and in November, 1895 the indictment against Cashin was dismissed on the grounds that there was insufficient evidence to convict.[218]

During his brief residency at 1607 Taylor D'Arcy Cashin was the secretary, and probably part owner, of a mining development company, the Maple Leaf, headquartered in British Columbia. A decade later his son Thomas Cashin achieved distinction as the first superintendent of San Francisco's Municipal Railway, the first municipal line in the United States. In 1912 Thomas oversaw the completion of MUNI's first line, on Geary Street, shortly before his untimely death at age thirty-eight.[219]

1607 Taylor closed out the pre-earthquake period under the ownership of Robert C. Clapp, a stockbroker from New York, and Agappita Osuna de Clapp, his Mexican-born wife. They resided in the house from 1902 to 1911 and then divided the house into flats. Under this family's long ownership (to 1946) the house was rented to artistic and literary people such as Sarah Bard Field, Maynard Dixon, Dorothea Lange, and Robert Boardman Howard.

The Jenks and Hanford Residences

Mr. Worcester tells me that, without exception, Mrs. Harvey's lot commands the finest views in the city and that it [the view] cannot be cut off. I was with him on the lot this morning and I quite agree with him. Joseph Britton's two lots are almost as good. If they do not possess a view quite as extensive, they have a slight advantage in location....

With the goat path up Vallejo Street properly converted into a series of terraces, and these lots properly improved, there could be no prettier place in San Francisco.

— Willis Polk, letter to Irving M. Scott, October 26, 1894, regarding the three 50-vara lots ultimately purchased by Livingston Jenks for his home at 1000 Vallejo[220]

As the pre-1906 chapter of the Summit's history drew to a close, two men planned new beginnings, both for themselves and for the neighborhood. In 1905, within a few months of each other, Livingston Jenks and Robert G. Hanford began construction of their residences at the northwest and southwest corners of Vallejo and Taylor streets. Simultaneously the stucco mansions rose up from the sandstone of Russian Hill, Jenks' residence directly across the street from Hanford's... and one could easily imagine that they regarded each other, vying for supremacy as the largest in the neighborhood. From the street the two houses looked like fortresses. In retrospect, their construction during 1905-1906 seems like twin acts of defiance, as if they were designed to withstand the coming firestorm.

The larger of the houses was probably that of attorney Livingston Jenks, at 1000 Vallejo. He purchased a huge site to build his house on: the three 50-vara lots of Britton and Harvey

referred to by Polk in the letter above, and a twelve foot sliver of land from Emilie Marshall adjoining the Worcester residence. Slightly over half the block belonged to Jenks by September, 1905.[221] Of course, only a fraction of this property was necessary to build on. Jenks chose the northwest corner of Vallejo and Taylor as his residence site. It was lower in elevation than the Worcester cottage next door, because Joseph Britton had performed extensive grading operations here (and on the lot to the north) in the mid-1870s. Nevertheless, the house, placed just behind Britton's stone retaining wall, rose high above Taylor Street.

Jenks chose a Los Angeles architect, Myron Hunt, and gave him complete artistic control. Hunt chose to design and situate the

Livingston Jenks residence, looking north at the south facade, 1906. *Architectural Record.*

Livingston Jenks residence, 1906. In this view we are looking NW from Vallejo and Taylor toward the south and east facades. *Architectural Record.*

house so that it blended with the exposed sandstone of the hill. Further excavation was avoided as much as possible. Because a bluff on which the house was built ran at an angle to the street, so the house would, too. When the concrete foundations were poured, even the lichens on the rock were protected with tarpaulins. The finished stucco walls of the house appeared to rise out of the natural rock in places, so closely did the two surfaces blend. The house was meant to look good on the brink of a cliff, and so the cliff was disturbed as little as possible.

Hunt reportedly drew inspiration from Tyrolean houses with which he was familiar, and so the Jenks residence, according to the *Architectural Record,"* has been made,

At left: Interior, Livingston Jenks residence, 1906. *Architectural Record.*

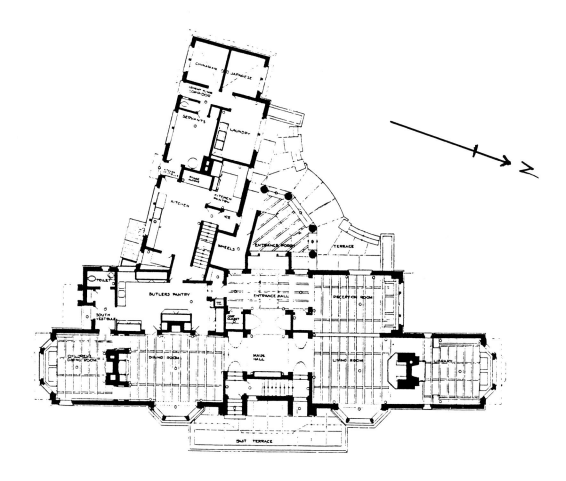

Livingston Jenks residence, first floor plan. *Architectural Record.*

consequently, somewhat rugged and substantial in appearance, with large plain wall surfaces, heavy projections, and an absence of any incongruous refinements."[222] The house was close in spirit to Worcester's design philosophy, although its surface material was different from the wood shingles that Worcester preferred.

The plan was irregular, with a main wing running roughly north-south, overlooking Taylor Street, and a service wing extending to the west at an eighty degree angle to the main. A broad entrance porch and courtyard filled the angle.

The interior had rooms ranging in size from small to cavernous, finished variously with wood and plaster. Large openings without doors or moldings connected the common rooms, which merged into one another, the plaster walls gradually changing colors from yellow, to bronze-yellow, to green. The paints were mixed by Hunt himself, who made sure the transitions were seamless. In the center of the house was an open space rising two stories to a balustraded musicians' gallery.

The entire west wing was devoted to support systems. There was a kitchen, a butler's pantry, a laundry room, a large room for Caucasian servants, and, at the extreme end, smaller living quarters for the Chinese and Japanese servants.

Vehicular access ran through the block from Green Street, with parking in a garage by the entrance porch. The Jenks residence must have been one of the first houses in the city designed with the automobile in mind. It appears to have been completed very shortly before the earthquake and fire.[223]

The Robert G. Hanford house at 1001 Vallejo was begun a few months before the Jenks house and was still under construction when the latter was finished. Three stories in height, with an attic and a large basement story, it was built to the property line on both Taylor and Vallejo streets, looming ponderously over passersby. Like the Jenks house, Hanford's was finished in stucco. The material had often been used as a smooth veneer for brick commercial and institutional buildings in San Francisco during the 1850s and 1860s, but had virtually never been used on residences until the 1890s, and rarely then. Its use on the Jenks and Hanford houses in 1905-1906 prefigured the stucco Mediterranean and pueblo houses that Horatio and Norman Livermore would build on Russian Hill Place, Florence Street, and Jones Street in 1912-1916.

Though built with similar materials, the two mansions looked quite different. Jenks' residence was southern European in feeling, while Hanford's had a more northern European look. The oriel windows were Tudorish, and crenelated at the top, with molded supports below. The squared-off gable facing Vallejo similarly conveyed a Tudor or medieval feeling. The windows were everywhere composed of many lights divided by leaded muntins, and made with a fine craftsmanship. The entrance, which faced Vallejo Street and was reached via the goat path, was somewhat classical in style. There was a conservatory with a separate entrance down the hill on Taylor Street, where

Robert G. Hanford residence, 1001 Vallejo. Photo ca. 1990 by author.

the north half of the Ranlett house had once stood. Although the house had many fine details, it was bulky in feeling, with projecting bays overhanging the sidewalk as if straining to expand the envelope of the building. In sum, it was less sophisticated and elegant than the Jenks house across the street. Its architect was Houghton Sawyer, who was then at the beginning of his career as a designer of fine residences and luxury apartment buildings.[224]

The owner, Robert G. Hanford, was a businessman and a mining promoter who, like Horatio P. Livermore, operated on a larger scale than most of his contemporaries even dreamed of. He made a fortune in 1901-1902 when he acquired control of several large street railways in San Francisco and, with Tirey L. Ford, engineered their sale to an eastern syndicate for a vastly inflated sum. This consolidation of the Market Street Railway, Sutter Street Railway, and an interurban line as the United Railroads was called the biggest cash deal in the history of the nation. At the same time, Hanford was active as a miner, dredging huge areas of the American and Feather rivers for gold deposits. He would later become active in electrical power and real estate.

Mrs. Hanford was a daughter of the founder of the Guittard Company, importers and dealers in tea, spices, coffee, soda, flavoring extracts, and especially chocolate. As Gabrielle Guittard Cavalsky she first met Hanford at the Del Monte golf course, where she was playing a round. As the *Call* later described, "In her outdoor costume, her cheeks aglow from open air exercise, her soft hair flying in the wind, she made a picture...." It was a picture that Hanford fell for utterly. Unfortunately, before they could marry, they each had to obtain a divorce. This they did in 1905. Hanford informed his wife by letter that "a man feels the grand passion but once in a lifetime," and "I have it for Mrs. Cavalsky." Shortly afterward, Gabrielle obtained her divorce from dentist Valdamar Cavalsky.[225]

Now Hanford could build a mansion for his new bride on the Summit of Russian Hill. The most notable feature of the house may have been designed with her in mind. It was a huge wood paneled ballroom at one end of which was an elevated balcony. According to a later resident, the new Mrs. Hanford was an accomplished vocalist, and she was to sing from this balcony accompanied by musicians below.[226]

The marriage would prove to be very short-lived, but no one knew that as the house neared completion and the couple prepared to move in. Scaffolding was up and finishing touches were being made to the exterior as the calendar page turned to April 18th.

Frank W. Demerest

Enough of mansions; let us conclude this chapter of Russian Hill history with the modest residences that stood in the small block bounded by Florence, Broadway, Vallejo and Jones streets. In particular, we shall return to Frank Demerest, who made a brief appearance earlier in these pages and will also figure in a later volume.

The days of some of these houses were numbered. Most of them were only one story in height, and all of them were considered architecturally out-of-date. Elsewhere on Russian Hill similar houses were having stories added to them or were being replaced by buildings of two or three flats. As plans by Willis Polk progressed for a formal entrance to the Summit at Vallejo and Jones, similar development pressures were being brought to bear upon the houses west of Florence Street. Norman Livermore had just purchased one of them, and he intended to replace it with a stable for his family. John McGaw, a realtor who lived at 1020 Green, had just purchased three of the houses and demolished one; he undoubtedly planned new development.

Such speculative plans aside, life went on much as before. Several of the houses were owner-occupied, and the rest were occupied by renters. The population was largely blue collar, moderately prosperous, and composed largely of immigrants, especially from Germany. The aging carpenter Peter Lowrey still lived at 1035 Vallejo, as he had since 1879. Other turn-of-the-century residents of this little block included

Looking north on Jones Street at the northeast corner of Broadway and Jones, 1890s. The second stories of the Demerest and Peter Lundberg (formerly Nagle) residences are visible on Broadway, peeking over the roof in the foreground. On the east side of Jones are a few small houses stranded high above the street as a result of street grading in 1870. Note the retaining walls in front. The empty lot on the corner was not developed until after 1906. The Marshall houses stand out on the horizon at right. California Historical Society.

William Earhardt, a gasfitter of German parentage (1041 Vallejo); Ernest Steake, a Geman carpenter (1043 Vallejo); Emil Geiter, a watchmaker for Shreve and Co. (1718 Jones); Robert Quinn, a machinist from Pennsylvania (1716 Jones); Henry Bruenn, a German miller (5 Florence) who would build a shanty out of fence boards after the 1906 fire destroyed his rented home; George Comstock, a janitor (5 1/2 Florence); Gustave Muller, an engineer or machinist (9 Florence); and Philip Hoffmann, a German linotype operator (11 Florence) who after the fire built a fine shingled house which no longer stands.

At 1080 Broadway, built in 1853 by George Nagle, the Summit's only known black residents lived briefly as renters. These were Geraldo G. Lyon, a native of Africa who worked as a cook and steward on the steamer *Gypsy*, and his wife Elizabeth, who was from the West Indies. They had two California-born children and a stepchild, and lived here from 1900-1902.

Next door, at 1078 Broadway, lived the Demerest family, which had built the house in 1863. James H. Demerest had worked the last decades of his life as a bill collector and died here in 1899 at age eighty, while his wife Phoebe died in about 1905 at age eighty-six. Their son Frank, who had been born in the gold country and grew to adulthood in this house, stayed on after his parents died.

After high school Frank Demerest went into his father's line of work, becoming a rent collector for Madison and Burke in the 1870s. Much later he recalled:

> I had the territory south of Market Street, and I went on horseback, carrying the rent money in my saddle bags. One time when I went down to the Royal Gimlet, a gambling house down on Howard Street, they tried to dope me so they could get my bags. Strong stuff? I'll say it was! But they didn't get me. I jumped on my horse before they

Frank Demerest, with friend. San Francisco History Archives.

> could stop me, and said "home" to that animal and he went.[227]

Demerest led a high life in those years. People who spoke of the "Gay '90s" didn't know Frank Demerest in the seventies and eighties. Dressed in a high hat, a cutaway coat, and fancy side burns, he hit all the spots. "I was a young daredevil then," he said.

> There wasn't anything — dances, lotteries, or anything else that was held, that I didn't go to. I was the first man that ever did the dip in San Francisco. I remember there was an affair one night at a place on Howard Street. I was dancing with Birdie when I took a notion to do something different, and I said to her, "Now watch me! We're going

to put a new step in this waltz." Birdie was all right. She just followed whatever I told her to do. All of a sudden we discovered that everyone else had stopped dancing and was watching us.[228]

Besides Birdie there was a woman named Eva, who Demerest said left a prominent pioneer for him. And apparently there was a marriage. At age eighty, he showed a reporter a newspaper clipping about an African tribesman aged 252 and living with his twenty-fourth wife. "I'll beat his record," Demerest said, "not the wife part, of course, one was enough for me."[229]

Demerest moved from Russian Hill to the South-of-Market area in about 1880 and lived there until about 1894, when he moved in with his parents again. They weren't particularly well off, but they seem to have had some property in the outlying parts of the city which Frank sold in later years.

One of the constants of his life, from his family's arrival on the Summit until his death, would be his curio collection. His collecting probably began during his childhood, as a result of the work he and his chums performed to earn money for fireworks. Beginning months before July 4th, he gathered rags, bottles, sacks and other junk in competition with the professional "ragpickers" and sold them to recyclers. He may have accumulated his youthful treasures during this scavenging process, and the Demerest basement became Frank's curio room. By the turn of the century he had collected an impressive pile of old plates and pots, music recordings, American flags, etc.

He found a marshal's or sheriff's badge and took to wearing it daily, pinned to his vest. He kept that badge for several decades.

Shortly after the turn of the century Demerest seems to have found a new romantic partner. Horatio P. Livermore referred to a resident of the Demerest house at this time as simply the "French woman," and a photograph from roughly the turn of the century shows Demerest standing next to a woman who may be her. Perhaps she thought his possessions were taking over the house, for in 1905 Demerest embarked upon a long project to create more room for his curios.

He found room for the stuff in an abandoned cistern on the property which had been used to collect rain water before the advent of Spring Valley water service. Ten feet wide and ten feet deep, it would serve admirably if one could get to it. It was, however, buried deeply in the sandstone of the hill, and so Demerest began to cut an opening into it with a hammer and chisel. Standing downhill from the top level of the cistern, Demerest cut through ten feet of rock before reaching the cistern's round brick wall. Then he cut through that. He finally had a V-shaped opening two-and-a-half feet wide at the bottom, five feet wide at the top, and ten feet in height. The project took nearly six months, and was finished in the second week of April, 1906.[230]

Demerest began to move his treasures into the round, brick-walled, cement-lined cistern. His timing could not have been more fortunate. He would ride out the coming fire storm in comparative comfort.

Here ends the first volume of this history of the Russian Hill neighborhood. Future volumes are planned which will complete the history of the entire hill, from the Russian graves that gave it its name to the high-rise battles of the 1960s.

INTERIOR · OF · CISTERN

MAKES · BEDROOM · OF · A · CISTERN

Frank Demerest's cistern, 1906. As a child Demerest had the reputation of owning more toys than anyone else in the neighborhood. He still did as a grown-up, and to hold them he converted the unused cistern on his property into a den. Demerest file, San Francisco History Archives, Main Library.

Notes

1. By one early source there were seven Russian graves, each surmounted by a black wooden cross. During the gold rush, the graveyard became a focus for informal burials of deceased 49ers. The graves were removed or built over during the 1850s. This topic will be discussed in a later volume on the history of Russian Hill.

2. George Livermore, "One Hundred Years of Livermore on Russian Hill," printed in Gardner W. Mein's real estate newsletter, 1990, in author's possession.

3. Mabel H. Collyer, "Russian, the Hill of Those Who Love It," *S. F. Call*, December 8, 1912 (Sunday section).

4. Arnold Genthe, *As I Remember*, p. 44.

5. Dawson, "A Gracious Visitation," *An Itinerant House and Other Stories*, pp. 141, 150, 207.

6. Wheeler, *Land Titles of San Francisco*, Schedule E (lots 810, 811, 840, 841, 850, 851). Gillespie and Gray, "Information from an Abstract of Title and Certificate of Search of Lot 810." Deeds (Old Series), Vol. 18, p. 631.

7. Homer Papers

8. Charles Homer, letter to Maria Homer, 1849, in the Homer Papers

9. Paul, "My First Two Years in California," p. 44.

10. Rasmussen, *San Francisco Ship Passenger Lists*, Vol. II, pp. 116-117.

11. SFD 1854, p. 236.

12. Homer, Cash Book and Ledger. These schools are illustrated in an undated [1850s] map, Britton and Rey, lithographers, "Public Buildings — San Francisco" at CHS.

13. Homer, Cash Book and Ledger. These have many entries under Ranlett (1851-1854) and Atkinson (1853-1854), and twelve entries under the partnership of "Homer, Ranlett and Atkinson" (1853-1854). There are also many entries under "Russian Hill Real Estate" (1853-1854).

14. Cincinnati City Directories 1842-1849. Censuses of 1860-1880.

15. Rasmussen, *San Francisco Ship Passenger Lists,* Vol. 1, pp. 21-23.

16. Deeds Vol. 35, p. 121.

17. Muhlberger, unpublished monograph on Ranlett sent to this author. See also Muhlberger, "William H. Ranlett, 19th Century Architect and Publisher."

18. The Greek revival, with its classical vocabulary, its symmetry, and restraint, was essentially a formal style. Davis and Downing, by their introduction of several picturesque and asymmetrical styles, were being anti-formal. The medieval and exotic styles and the rustic settings they chose can be thought of as fitting in with Romantic philosophy as it developed in early 19th century Europe. See Scully, *The Shingle Style and the Stick Style* on this transformation in the United States.

19. Ibid.

20. A set of *The Architect* can be found in the Environmental Design Library, University of California, Berkeley.

21. Muhlberger, "William H. Ranlett, 19th-Century Architect and Publisher."

22. Haskins, *The Argonauts of California*, p. 478.

23. Ranlett and Co., "Map of Sonoma," 1850. Map Room, University of California, Berkeley.

24. Garnett, ed., *Papers of the San Francisco Committee of Vigilance of 1851*, Vol. 1, p. 33, lists Ranlett as a member.

25. Hammond, ed., *The Larkin Papers*, Vol. 9, p.16 and p. 157.

26. SFD 1854, p. 111 and adv. dept. p. 21. For an illustration of the Italianate style Custom House Block, see *The Annals of San Francisco*, p. 473.

27. Homer's surviving Cash Book and Ledger, at the Bancroft Library, lists twelve entries for this partnership, but unfortunately does not give locations or further particulars.

28. *Alta* Nov. 9, 1857, p. 2. *Chronicle* Feb. 16, 1919 (also in Morphy, *S. F. Thoroughfares*, "Russian Hill," p. 52).

29. Swasey, *Early Days and Men of California*, pp. 385-396. Sullivan, *Early Days in California*, pp. 212-215. *Alta*, March 18, 1864, p. 1, col. 2.

30. Deeds Vol. 35, Sept. 16, 1853.

31. General Index Vol. 6, Homer to Morrison, deed, May 6, 1854. Since the corresponding Deed book is missing, one must identify the property in question by using General Index and Deed volumes to trace the subsequent ownership (e.g. General Index Vol. 11, Morrison, dec'd, to Horace Muzzy, deed, Feb. 1858; Deeds Vol. 154, Muzzy to Peter G. Partridge, March 1862).

32. General Index Vols. 7 and 9: lien transactions under Morrison's name suggest he worked as a contractor.

33. These residents were found in census and city directory listings.

34. The facts of the case are summarized in Cyril V. Gray, Counsel, "Appellant's Brief: In the Supreme Court of the State of California, George D. Nagle vs. Charles Homer," 1857.

35. SFD 1858-1862, etc. Charles Homer is no longer listed in directories after 1861.

36. In 1910 Lillian and Ethel demolished 1601 Taylor and built new houses on the lot for their families, 1020 Broadway and 1629 Taylor, both extant.

37. *Lone Mountain Cemetery Records,* Book 1, at the Society of California Pioneers. *San Francisco Cemetery Records, 1848-1863* (1938). *Records from Laurel Hill Cemetery, 1853-1937.* The latter two are typescripts that may be found at the San Francisco History Archives, Main Library.

38. Nathaniel Gray's undertaking establishment is still in business today on Sutter Street as Halstead-N. Gray-Carew and English.

39. *Alta* Nov. 27, 1853, p. 2; Nov. 28; Nov. 30, p. 2; April 1, 1854, p. 2; June 13, adv. on p. 5. Lone Mountain Cemetery was dug up in the 1930s and replaced by the offices of Fireman's Fund Insurance Co. A bronze plaque on the south side of California Street, just west of Presidio Boulevard, marks the spot, but makes no mention of the proprietors.

40. Nathaniel Gray, biographical material, folder 6, Bancroft Library.

41. General Index Vol. 7, Ranlett to Atkinson, deed, Dec. 27, 1854. In subsequent General Indexes Atkinson, not Ranlett, is listed as a proprietor of Lone Mountain Cemetery.

42. The Ranlett's purchased an old Dutch house in Ho-Ho-Kus, New Jersey, near Adelaide's home town. William built his practice up again, regaining much of his wealth and social position. Strongly pro-North during the Civil War, he designed a Union Hall for the Republicans, and he armed twenty-five men at his own expense to defend his church's Union flag from Southern sympathizers. Ranlett's old Vigilance Committee friends would have applauded his style. His life ended in double tragedy. One of his sons was killed in the war, and when the body was returned by funeral train, Ranlett had to make plans for its burial. On one such errand, Ranlett's horse became startled, throwing Ranlett to the ground and killing him. He and his son were buried together on November 12, 1865. Muhlberger, "William H. Ranlett..." an unpublished monograph.

43. *Records from Tombstones in Laurel Hill Cemetery.* 1880 census. *Chronicle* July 8, 1880, p. 8, col. 7 (death notice).

44. Paul's life is chronicled in a published article that he wrote, "My First Two Years in California," *Quarterly of the Society of California Pioneers,* and in his unpublished reminiscences, "Biographical Sketch of the Life of Almarin B. Paul, written by Himself" (1879-1883), at CHS. The former is a very lively, humorous, and well-written account, while the latter is more revealing of his inner life. See also Hall, "Diary of a Trip from Ione to Nevada in 1859," in CHSQ, p. 80, note 16.

45. He later developed a roster of pennames for his writing for various newspapers: "Clarence," "Almarin," "Junious, Jr.," and "An Old Californian."

46. SFD 1856 shows Paul and Rhodes living at "Broadway near Taylor."

47. Rhodes is one of those characters out of history who keeps surfacing as a footnote from time to time. Although he became a district court commissioner, wrote innumerable political editorials under the penname "Caxton," and was frequently asked to contribute poems for solemn occasions, his chief fame has been as a science fiction writer, for which practice he neglected his law career. A collection of his stories, *Caxton's Book,* was published upon his death in 1876 by his friends. It was reprinted with an introduction by the science fiction historian Sam Moskowitz in the 1970s, and in 1980 Moskowitz devoted a chapter to Rhodes in his book *The History of the Movement* (pp. 43-61), on Victorian science fiction writers in San Francisco. The seance which Rhodes and Paul participated in at the Manrow house on Russian Hill (see a later volume in this Russian Hill history) has also been resurrected from time to time. A revealing indicator of Rhodes's outré tastes is that he named his son Arthur Pym, after the main character in Edgar Allan Poe's only novel. See also Shuck, *History of the Bench and Bar,* pp. 545-547; Wheat, "California's Bantam Cock," in CHSQ Sept. 1931, p. 266, note 64; and

Walker, *San Francisco's Literary Frontier.*

48. Regarding Paul's silver ore reduction mill, see Lord, *Comstock Mining and Miners*, pp. 84-88; Lyman, *Saga of the Comstock Lode*, pp. 60, 70, 144-146 of the paperback edition; Sam P. Davis, ed., *History of Nevada* (n.d.), Vol. 1, pp. 334, 350, 626; and Smith, *History of the Comstock Lode*, pp., 17, 41-42. I have not sought out Paul's own articles (as by "Cosmos") in the *Bulletin* June 30, 1860, p. 1, col. 1; Nov. 1, 1861, p. 1; April 10 and 27, 1863; Oct. 22, 1863; May 25, 1864, p. 1; among no doubt others.

49. Kast, "Declaration of Agnes Kast" (1977) states that Twain was a visitor here. Agnes Kast had lived at 1069 and 1073 Broadway and knew Kate Atkinson, the Paul sisters, and Ina Coolbrith.

50. See Lyman, *Saga of the Comstock Lode*, pp. 298-307, for an extended account.

51. Neider, ed., *Selected Letters of Mark Twain*, p. 46. See also Twain's references to Paul (1864) in Branch, et. al., ed., *Mark Twain's Letters*, Vol. 1, pp. 274 and 282.

52. Paul, "Biographical Sketch...,"pp. 231-237.

53. REC Jan. 1871, p. 3, col. 1.

54. 1880 census.

55. Paul, "Biographical Sketch...," pp. 241-243.

56. Cornwall later became one of the Bay Area's major industrialists. For Alvinza Hayward and D. O. Mills, owners of the Black Diamond coal mine at Mt. Diablo and the Bellingham Bay Coal Company in Washington Territory, Cornwall served as the agent and later president of these companies. He developed railroad and steamship lines as far north as British Columbia to service these and other mines. In 1880-1881 he became vice-president and treasurer, then president of the new California Electric Light Co., which bought coal from Cornwall's Black Diamond mine. When it stopped doing so. Cornwall left to form his own electric company, which did well, and eventually merged with PG&E. Cornwall died in 1904. Coleman, *P. G. and E. of California*; Cornwall, *Life and Sketch of Pierre Barlow Cornwall.* Swasey, *Early Days and Men of California*, pp. 250-253.

57. *Examiner*, Nov. 20, 1898, p. 11, col. 2 (obit. of Theller)

58. *Municipal Reports* of 1866 shows the street was graded in that year.

59. Deeds 154, p. 247. REC May 1874 and Jan. 1875; SFNL Jan. 16, 1875; General Index 103, May 5, 1879, Partridge to Wood. SFD 1860s-1870s for Turner and Partridge. Great Register 1867-1873 for Turner. 1870 census.

60. Deeds 96, p. 468. Deeds 194, p. 225. *Argonaut* Nov. 29, 1924. City directory and census listings.

61. City directories of 1862-1863 refer to a John Owen, tailor, who lived on the east side of Jones between Vallejo and Green, but nothing more definite is known of this resident and his dwelling.

62. *Marysville Daily Appeal*, Feb. 15, 1862 (in Richard N. Schellens Papers, p. 539, at CHS). *Alta California*, Sept. 17, 1862, p. 1, col. 2. "Around Russian Hill," *Examiner*, Nov. 24, 1889, p. 8, col. 2. *Bancroft's Tourist Guide*, p. 180. Morphy, *San Francisco Thoroughfares*, vol. 2, p. 65-66. Roger Jobson, telephone interview by the author, 1987.

63. "Beautifying Our City," *Bulletin*, March 2, 1876, p. 2, col. 3. "Excelsior" misidentified the site as being "bounded by Taylor, Jones, Filbert and Greenwich streets, I think," but that block was much lower, and packed with houses.

64. Joseph Britton was a printer and lithographer who had lived at the southeast corner of Union and Taylor since 1855. He was also a city supervisor and active in building cable car lines, including Hallidie's first line and one on Union Street over Russian Hill. His story will be told in a later volume covering the East Slope.

65. Britton had purchased the two 50-vara lots facing Taylor in 1875, soon after Margaret Richards left her house. Some time afterward he purchased the middle 50-vara lot on the south side of Green Street, thus owning half the block. He probably demolished both the Richards and Stratman houses to make way for his unrealized development plans.

66. SFNL Jan. 8, 1870, G. Palache to D. P. Marshall, this lot, for $2000.

67. Dillon, *Iron Men*, p. 97.

68. *A Brief Account of the Institution of the San Francisco Society of the New Jerusalem.*

69. Emanuel Swedenborg (1688-1772), Swedish and a lifelong Lutheran, pursued a wide-ranging scientific career until the age of fifty-six. He made substantial contributions in the areas of mining, metallurgy, astronomy, and mathematics; promoted inventions of his own; and did significant anatomical research, particularly of the brain and glands. In 1743, he claimed, he began to have visions, dreams, and visits to the afterlife, where he

conversed with human spirits in the form of angels. He made very specific descriptions of the afterlife, how it functioned, and the method by which a person enters heaven or hell. In many ways his writings of his experiences depart from traditional Christianity. He devoted the last thirty years of his life to his religious writing, which covers over thirty volumes. Twelve years after his death his followers founded the Church of the New Jerusalem, or New Church, which grew to a large membership in the nineteenth century. Joseph Worcester's brothers were preeminent scholars in this field.

70. Alfred Worcester, "Rev. Joseph Worcester, A Memoir and Extracts...." Alfred says that Joseph was ordained in Waltham Chapel on November 3 and left for San Francisco in 1868. A pamphlet printed by the church in 1870, however, says that Joseph arrived in December, 1867.

71. Alfred Worcestor, "Rev. Joseph Worcester, A Memoir and Extracts."

72. James F. Lawrence, "Working Draft of an Essay on Joseph Worcester."

73. Freudenheim and Sussman, *Building With Nature*, p. 10. The authors make reference to letters by Worcester regarding this house that I have not seen.

74. For illustrations (two photos and a William Keith painting), see Freudenheim and Sussman, *Building With Nature*, pp. 8-9. For their suggestion that Worcester was inspired by an early trip to Yosemite, where he saw the Hutchings house and other rustic cabins, see pp. 10-11. The Worcester house was moved to 575 Blair Avenue early this century and thoroughly remodeled. Though still shingled, Worcester's house no longer resembles its early appearance.

75. Freudenheim and Sussman, *Building With Nature*, p. 7.

76. These include two volumes of plates of H. H. Richardson's Trinity Church and Ames Memorial building (1870s), two volumes of photos of buildings in Venice and Florence, three of Italian religious paintings, two of miscellaneous subjects (including English Gothic churches, medieval buildings, and American homes), and later subjects: the Phoebe Hearst plan for the University of California, and the *Architectural Record* (1901-1905). When Worcester acquired the earlier material is unknown. Worcester Collection, DOCS.

77. The classic, and essential, treatise on this style, and its evolution from earlier ones, is Vincent Scully, Jr.'s *The Shingle Style and the Stick Style*.

78. The Coleman-Specht house is illustrated in *Victorian Classics of San Francisco*, Windgate Press (1987), plate 25 (reprinted from SFNL's Artistic Homes series). The Howard house in San Mateo is the subject of Price's own book, *A Country House in California*, which can be found at DOCS.

79. Considering Worcester's finances and modes of transportation, it is unlikely that he ever traveled to San Mateo to see the Howard house.

80. Historian Woodruff C. Minor questions this assessment. If one judges Worcester's houses by the pastor's desire to design in accordance with nature, rather than in an attempt to fit in with an east coast architectural style, then his Piedmont house of 1877 is more successful than his Russian Hill houses of 1888-1889.

81. CABN October, 1888 lists a building contract identifying the "architect" simply as "Wooster." The WD hookup date was Jan. 7, 1889.

82. McEnerney Judgment #9334 (County Clerk's Office, City Hall) confirms the story that Worcester received a lifetime lease from the Marshalls. Alfred Worcester, letter to Edmund Sears, 1930, states that Emilie Marshall built Worcester's house. James F. Lawrence, "Working Draft..." states that Worcester received funds from a family trust.

83. Woodruff C. Minor suggests that the similarities between these two houses indicates Worcester's deep affection for the lost Piedmont house and his desire to perpetuate it, with its hillside setting, on Russian Hill.

84. *California Art Research*, Vol. 5, pp. 16-31. Both quotes are from this source. Brother Cornelius, *Keith, Old Master*, p. 16. *Chronicle*, Nov. 2, 1931 (obit.). Hughes, *Artists in California*, p. 386. See the latter for locations of works by Richardson.

85. Brother Cornelius, *Keith, Old Master*, p. 434. See Keeler, *Friends Bearing Torches*, p. 37, for a similar example.

86. Brother Cornelius, *Keith, Old Master*, p. 435.

87. See, for instance, Brother Cornelius, *Keith, Old Master*, p. 363.

88. Richard C. Cabot, letter to Mrs. Arthur (Susie) Lyman, July, 1901.

89. The drawing is from the *Examiner*, Sept. 30, 1895.

90. Keeler, *Friends Bearing Torches*, p. 38; Cabot, letter to Lyman; Alfred Worcester, "Rev. Joseph Worcester, A Memoir and Extracts," and Murdock, *A Backward Glance at Eighty*, p. 241 all write of Worcester's hospitality and mention the same menu.

91. Sears, "Joseph Worcester," a memoir, June, 1930.

92. Ibid.

93. Keeler, *Friends Bearing Torches*, p. 36.

94. Murdock, *A Backward Glance at Eighty*, pp. 241-242.

95. Alfred Worcester, "Rev. Joseph Worcester, A Memoir and Extracts."

96. Brother Cornelius, *Keith, Old Master*, pp. 361-362.

97. Ibid., pp. 362, 374.

98. Steffens, *Autobiography*, p. 552.

99. Ibid., p. 553.

100. See for instance his letter to John Galen Howard regarding design on the UC campus in 1902, quoted in Freudenheim and Sussman, *Building With Nature*, p. 7, note 1.

101. Steffens, *Autobiography*, p. 553.

102. At DOCS.

103. One of Wood's renters is known: Robert Flenniken, the owner of a dry goods store at 724-726 Montgomery Street (an extant building in today's Jackson Square). He lived in the Morrison-Turner-Partridge house during 1884-1886.

104. Brother Cornelius, *Keith, Old Master*, p. 362.

105. This story is collected in the "SF Streets" scrapbook, vol. 5, of Morphy's "S. F. Thoroughfares" column, CHS.

106. George Livermore, interview by William Kostura, March 30, 1988.

107. Polk's *Architectural News* shows Polk living in Oakland in Nov. 1890. He is known to have moved to Russian Hill by Dec. 1891. The date can be narrowed further. In March 1891 Polk was remodeling a house for Dr. William Boericke, who was a parishioner of Worcester's at the Church of the New Jerusalem. Polk probably met Boericke through the pastor, which suggests that Polk and Worcester were neighbors by then.

108. Edward O'Day, "Varied Types — Willis Polk," in *Town Talk*, Feb. 25, 1911, p. 7.

109. Longstreth, *On the Edge of the World*, pp. 51-56. This book is a masterpiece of research using primary sources from across the nation.

110. George Livermore, interview by William Kostura, March 30, 1988. Longstreth, *On the Edge of the World*, p. 372, note 12.

111. A set of this periodical can be found at DOCS.

112. After the third issue Polk tried without success to sell stock in the *Architectural News*, claiming the magazine had funds to cover the next quarter of a year. He also proposed a merger with *California Architect and Building News*, with CABN assuming AN's $730 debt, and Polk as editor. Polk Papers, DOCS

113. *The Wave*, Dec. 19, 1891.

114. Peixotto, "Architecture in San Francisco," *Overland Monthly*, May 1893, pp. 449-463.

115. *Architectural News*, Nov. 1890 mentions a meeting. Longstreth, *On the Edge of the World*, p. 2, has a photo.

116. *The Wave*, Aug. 8, 1891, p. 2, Dec. 5, 1891, pp. 1-2. *Call* April 10, 1892, p. 12, col. 3, with a drawing of the building by Dan Polk.

117. Longstreth, *On the Edge of the World*, p. 428. Illustrated in CABN May 1894, del. by Dan Polk.

118. The S. F. Art Association met in the former Mark Hopkins mansion on Nob Hill and was the forerunner of today's S. F. Art Institute. Virgil Williams, as its first director, was extremely influential among local artists. He died in 1886.

119. McEnerney Judgment (Quiet Title) #22005 documents the sale of the 40' lot to Dora Williams in July, 1892. *S. F. Call* Jan. 11, 1893, p. 5, col. 6 documents the late recording of Brown's sale of the 20' lot to Polk. An old story, apparently false, is that Mrs. Williams gave the 20' lot to the Polks in exchange for Willis Polk's architectural services.

120. Longstreth, *On the Edge of the World*, pp. 118-119.

121. Morphy, "San Francisco Thoroughfares," S. F. Streets scrapbook, vol. 5, CHS.

122. Longstreth, *On the Edge of the World*, pp. 232-234. Guild stationary in the Polk Papers, DOCS, lists directors.

123. See his several drawings published in CABN during the mid-1890s.

124. *Chronicle*, October 26, 1892, p. 10, col. 1.

125. *The Wave*, August 13, 1892.

126. Morphy, "San Francisco Thoroughfares," S. F. Streets scrapbook, vol. 5, CHS.

127. *Call*, July 13, 1893, p. 2, col. 5.

128. Brother Cornelius, *Keith, Old Master*, pp. 351-352; p. 596, note 17.

129. Collected in Longstreth, *A Matter of Taste*.

130. *Call* July 20, 1893.

131. *Call* July 23, 1893, p. 15, col. 2.

132. *Call* February 13, 1896, p. 11, col. 6.

133. Mizner, *The Many Mizners*. Mizner later became the society architect of Palm Springs, Florida. His Spanish, Moorish, and generally Mediterranean houses of the 1910s and 1920s have undergone a revival of interest.

134. *Call*, August 21, 1896, p. 5, col. 7; August 26, p. 5, col. 2; August 29, p. 9, col. 3. The newspaper's evident delight at reporting Polk's difficulties should be kept in mind when assessing these events. In general, the *Examiner* and the *Wave* were favorable toward Polk, while the *Call* was critical.

135. *Call* July 31, 1897, p. 9, col. 4.

136. Longstreth, *On the Edge of the World*, pp. 176-177. The mine grounds are now owned by the State of California and are open to the public.

137. These projects are illustrated in Longstreth, *On the Edge of the World*, pp. 224, 234, 236, 242.

138. E. H. Hamilton, "The City of St. Francis," *Examiner*, Jan. 28, 1894, p. 60.

139. Longstreth, *On the Edge of the World*, pp. 235, 243.

140. *Chronicle*, Dec. 16, 1899, p. 12, col. 5.

141. This date, from his last city directory listing, is highly uncertain.

142. Longstreth, *On the Edge of the World*, p. 372, note 14.

143. Polk Papers, DOCS

144. Brother Cornelius, *Keith, Old Master*, p. 596, note 18. This story was told to Brother Cornelius by Mrs. H. P. Livermore.

145. Thompson, "The Early Domestic Architecture..."

146. Freudenheim and Sussman, *Building With Nature*, p. 30, note 5. The authors consulted Charles Moore, *Daniel Burnham: Architect, Planner of Cities* (1921).

147. Previously, in 1901, after the death of George Percy, Worcester suggested to Burnham that he take Willis Polk into his employ in Chicago. Burnham agreed, and Polk spent two years there broadening his career. Polk must have impressed Burnham, for when Polk returned to San Francisco in 1903 it was as the chief designer of D. H. Burnham and Co., a western branch of the Chicago firm. One of his first San Francisco projects under Burnham was the fourteen story Merchants' Exchange Building on California Street (extant).

148. Keeler, *Friends Bearing Torches*, pp. 36-37.

149. Burnham, letter to Keith, ca. Dec. 1907, in Brother Cornelius, *Keith, Old Master*, p. 479.

150. *Scientific American*: Building Edition, vol. 28, no. 2 (August 1899), p. 35.

151. Richard C. Cabot, letter to Mrs. Arthur Lyman, July 24, 1901.

152. Joseph Worcester, letter to Alfred Worcester, March 1, 1892, in Alfred Worcester, "Rev. Joseph Worcester: A Memoir and Extracts." Woodruff C. Minor feels that this quote indicates Worcester was a "primitivist" who would have been repelled by elaborate or ostentatious designs. This disapproval would apply even to east coast shingle style houses, with their richly carved wooden interiors demanded by a wealthy clientele. Minor feels that Worcester's Piedmont cottage and the Swedenborgian Church designs emanate from this same

impulse. The point is that Worcester was hardly influenced by the "eastern" shingle style at all, but rather developed an architectural philosophy based on his personal values.

153. Richard C. Cabot, letter to Mrs. Arthur Lyman, July 24, 1901.

154. Freudenheim and Sussman, *Building With Nature*, pp. 20-31. On page 21, note 33 they discuss Porter's role. Longstreth, *On the Edge of the World*, p. 389, note 28, discovered Schweinfurth's role in the design and generally discounts Brown's importance. See also Brother Cornelius, *Keith, Old Master*, pp. 366-369.

155. Richard C. Cabot, letter to Mrs. Arthur Lyman, July 24, 1901.

156. Alfred Worcester, "Rev. Joseph Worcester: A Memoir and Extracts."

157. Murdock, *A Backward Glance at Eighty*, p. 241.

158. Brother Cornelius, *Keith, Old Master*, p. 370

159. Ibid., pp. 370-372. Brother Cornelius investigated this matter, but I am not convinced he did so thoroughly.

160. Richard C. Cabot, letter to Mrs. Arthur Lyman, July 24, 1901.

161. Kast, "Declaration of Agnes Kast." Kast lived at 1069 Broadway and then 1073 Broadway from 1910 to 1964.

162. SFNL May 4, 1872 documents Joseph Atkinson's gift to Kate of some of this land. Regarding her sale of the property, I have found a few deed abstracts in the *Chronicle*, Nov. 24, 1889; *Call* Aug. 14, 1891; and *Edward's Abstracts* Jan. 29 1895. There must be many more. She reinvested some of her income from the sale of this property by building a commercial storefront on Sutter Street that was designed for her by A. Page Brown. Illustrated in Longstreth, *On the Edge of the World*, p. 267.

163. *Chronicle* Jan. 25, 1870, p. 3; Jan. 28, p. 3; Jan. 29, p. 3; Jan. 30, p. 5.

164. Kate Atkinson, letter, 1886, Bancroft Library. *Call*, Oct. 24, 1887, p. 3, col. 4. SFD 1896-1897.

165. *Bulletin*, Dec. 27, 1858, p. 3, col. 2., re: Kate Atkinson and the Pioneer Sunday School. William H. Rhodes, until recently a boarder at the Atkinson house, wrote the poem that she read. See *Bulletin*, Feb. 16, 1891, p. 3, col. 4, for Maria Homer's obit. The Unitarian Church has some membership and pew rental records for the 1870s-1890s, including Maria Homer's and Kate Atkinson's.

166. All material on Burgess's life through 1890 (and much afterward) is from Joseph Backus, *Gelett Burgess*, a comprehensive dissertation at the Bancroft Library.

167. Backus, in *Gelett Burgess*, reports that Burgess suddenly struck Porter in the mouth at a party in London, an act for which he never explained or apologized.

168. Backus, *Gelett Burgess*, pp. 120-125.

169. Burgess, Diaries, 1891-1892.

170. Backus, *Gelett Burgess*, pp. 142-143.

171. Polk Papers, Cashbook, DOCS. Backus, *Gelett Burgess*, p. 140. According to Backus, the redwood paneling was carved by Swiss craftsmen under Polk's supervision. Several of William H. Ranlett's pedimented windows and doorways, enframed by classical pilasters, remain intact on the second floor.

172. Backus, *Gelett Burgess*, p. 140. Bruce Porter has also been given credit for this garden. How Atkinson's innumerable cats took to the new environment was not recorded.

173. Built in 1891, the Summerton was designed in a full-blown High Victorian style that Willis Polk must have hated. San Francisco's *true* Bohemian artists generally avoided such places, and Burgess moved away the following year.

174. Backus, *Gelett Burgess*, pp. 131, 133.

175. *Chronicle*, Sept. 15, 1889, p. 16.

176. SFD 1896; SFD 1897, p. 48. Burgess's floor plan of the house, in Notebook #20, Burgess Papers, is labeled "Russian Hill Neighborhood House." The alternate possible use of this house, as a neighborhood meeting place, seems unlikely.

177. Burgess, *Lady Méchante*, taken from Backus, "Gelett Burgess," pp. 134-135.

178. Backus, *Gelett Burgess*, pp. 135-136, 139-140.

179. Ibid., pp. 246-247.

180. *The Lark*, Jan. 1896.

181. Martinez, *Elsie Whitaker Martinez*, p. 227.

182. Ibid., pp. 150-151.

183. Mackay, The Violent Friend, p. 21.

184. Ibid., p. 469.

185. Ibid., p. 470.

186. Kast, "Declaration of Agnes Kast."

187. Backus, *Gelett Burgess*, p. 153. The Huntington Library in San Marino has one of these booklets and reprinted it in facsimile in 1968 as Burgess, *The Purple Cow and Other Poems.*

188. Burgess, letter to Inez Irwin, 1895, at Bancroft Library. Quoted in Backus, *Gelett Burgess*, p. 153.

189. *Epi-Lark*, May, 1897, p. 1. In Backus, *Gelett Burgess*, pp. 153-154.

190. It was quoted at him endlessly, and he wearied of it much as Ravel did of Bolero. In the last issue of *The Lark* Burgess wrote: "Ah yes, I wrote the 'Purple Cow'/ I'm Sorry, now, I wrote it/But I can tell you Anyhow/I'll Kill you if you Quote it!"

191. Porter, letter to James D. Hart, 1952, in Bancroft Library. Quoted in Backus, *Gelett Burgess*, p. 199.

192. Dixon's was a fine drawing of a moustachioed, goateed, cigarette smoking Spanish cowboy playing a guitar. The drawing bore a strong resemblance to how Dixon would himself look many years later. According to Backus, in *Gelett Burgess*, p. 200, Burgess uncharitably called the drawing a "blot on the scutcheon."

193. Quotes taken from Backus, *Gelett Burgess*, pp. 217, 242, 246.

194. Ibid., p. 241.

195. By all means, however, seek out *The Heart Line* (1907) and *The Picaroons* (1904), the latter written with Will Irwin. Both are set in pre-earthquake San Francisco, and both make excellent use of local scenes.

196. Bruce Porter, letter to Franklin Walker, 1930. In Backus, *Gelett Burgess*, p. 272.

197. Backus, *Gelett Burgess*, p. 265.

198. One of these residences, 1210-1212 Lombard, still stands. Burgess's story while living there will be taken up in a later volume.

199. Will Irwin was born in New York in 1873, graduated from Stanford in 1899, and became an editor at *The Wave* and the *Chronicle*. He lived at 1041 1/2 Vallejo, near Jones, during 1902-1903, and at 2548 Hyde in 1904. His brother Wallace Irwin, born in 1876, followed him to Stanford, and authored Lark-ish booklets "Love Sonnets of a Hoodlum" (1901) and "The Rubaiyat of Omar Kayyam, Jr.", both wildly popular. Wallace lived in Dora Williams' house, 1019 Vallejo, in 1902, and at 1625 Taylor (apparently a side entrance to one of the Polk flats) in 1903. Both Irwins went on to New York in or about 1904, about the time Burgess returned, and Will in particular became a very successful writer and editor. He authored *The City That Was* within hours after San Francisco burned in 1906, and wrote the text to Arnold Genthe's collection of photographs, *Pictures of Old Chinatown* (1908). He and Burgess shared an apartment and an 87' model railroad on East Twenty-third Street in New York City.

200. The estate was where the Claremont Country Club is today. George Livermore, interview by the author, April 7, 1988.

201. This story first appeared in Morphy, San Francisco Thoroughfares (in S.F. Streets Scrapbook, CHS, vol. 5).

202. Stone held a variety of clerical jobs while living at 1023 Vallejo. He became the proprietor of a parcel delivery service when he moved into 1036 Vallejo.

203. Drury, *The Livermore Family*. This manuscript, at the Bancroft Library, was written by a Livermore family friend.

204. Coleman, *P. G. & E. of California*, pp. 117-126. This is not an unbiased source, for it was commissioned by P. G. & E., of which Norman Livermore had long been a director.

205. Horatio P. Livermore's first wife was Mattie Banks, who died of tuberculosis in 1883. The eighty year employment of Lim Ti Ark by the Livermores must be a record of some sort.

206. George Livermore, interview by William Kostura, April 7, 1988.

207. These changes can be deduced from Sanborn insurance maps, old photographs, and an inspection of the house with George Livermore in the mid-1980s.

208. Coleman, *P. G. and E. of California*, p. 159. The original Folsom Dam no longer exists. It was supplanted by the current, much larger Folsom Dam, some distance downstream, construction of which began in 1948.

209. Biographical sketches of Norman Livermore can be found in *History of the Greater San Francisco Bay Region*, vol. 3, pp. 2-3; Allen L. Chickering, "In Memorium: Norman B. Livermore," in *California Historical Society Quarterly*, vol. 33, March, 1954, pp. 81-82; and Coleman, *P. G. and E. of California*, pp. 126-127.

210. *Edward's Abstracts from Records*, June 23, 1903, Building Contracts. Holmes had recently moved into one of Dora Williams flats at 1019 Vallejo.

211. The Gray Brothers firm that Horatio planned to hire was a major contractor responsible for much work in San Francisco, from concrete foundations for buildings to bridges in Golden Gate Park. Much of this work survives today. They were the same Gray Brothers notorious for dynamiting the cliffs on the east side of Telegraph Hill. Willis Polk's original design for the Vallejo Street improvements has not been found, but it was probably similar to the present stairway, ramps, and balustraded carriage turnaround built in 1914.

212. The *San Francisco Chronicle* and other papers pieced together the story of Morgan's life, amassed a list of his defrauded clients, and covered his disappearance and arrest over a nine day period from March 26 to April 3, 1897. For identities of Morgan's clients, see especially March 28. For the Edwin K. Alsip story, see especially March 31 and April 1. Follow-up stories were printed on April 10, 18, and 24.

213. The *Chronicle*, on April 1st, identified the infant as that of Louise Lindstrom, a domestic servant who had given it up, in the reporter's words, "to hide the living evidence of her shame." On April 3rd, the *Chronicle* revealed that Morgan had been born as Morgan Powell Morgan. He had changed his name to cover up earlier misdeeds. Eugenie Howell's real name was Miss E. Maybon. I have used the names by which Morgan was known in the 1890s and by which "Howell" was identified in most news articles.

214. Deeds vol. 1664, p. 145, Sept. 16, 1895.

215. Wilder, *West from Home*, p. 89. Roos, "Houses Out of San Francisco History." Jacques Schnier, interview by William Kostura, March 29, 1984. Schnier lived in the house during the 1940s-1950s and heard the story from a relative of an early resident of the house.

216. Extensive efforts on the author's part to find the moved portion of this house have failed.

217. Deeds, vol. 1765, p. 80.

218. *Examiner* Aug. 24, 1893, p. 6. *Call*, Aug. 20, 1895, p. 7, col. 3; Nov. 3, 1895, p. 13, col. 2.

219. Meyer, et. al., ed. *Municipal Blue Book*, p. 71. Obit, Pioneer Scrapbook A, p. 18, Society of California Pioneers.

220. Polk Papers, DOCS

221. McEnerney Judgment 32639, County Clerk's Office. Deeds 2036, p. 221, Marshall to Jenks, Jan. 1904. Deeds 2136, p. 178, Harvey to Jenks, Sept. 1905.

222. "A House on a Cliff: The Residence of Mr. Livingston Jenks," *Architectural Record*. The photographs used here are from this article.

223. The house was demolished in the 1950s. Its replacement is not remotely as sensitive to the special qualities of the site as was the Jenks house.

224. *Edward's Abstracts from Records* June 21, 1905. The completion of the house was recorded in EA July 3, 1906 (Acceptances), 2 1/2 months after the earthquake.

225. *Call* July 6, 1909, p. 2.

226. Jacques Schnier, interview by William Kostura, March 8, 1985. Schnier rented the conservatory first from Sally Stanford and then from the owner, Paul Verdier, during the late 1930s-early 1940s. In the 1950s the ballroom was divided into apartments. A few years ago the partitions were removed and the ballroom was restored, only to be destroyed soon afterward.

227. *Argonaut* (96) Nov. 29, 1924, p. 18.

228. Ibid.

229. McQuade, "Neighborhood Characters — Dad Demerest."

230. Newspaper clipping, Demerest file, SFHA.

Bibliography

A List of Abbreviations Used in Notes and Bibliography:

Bancroft	Bancroft Library, University of California, Berkeley
CABN	*California Architect and Building News*
Census	U. S. Census enumerations of 1860-1900
CHS	California Historical Society, San Francisco
CHSQ	*California Historical Society Quarterly, California History*
DOCS	Documents Collection, College of Environmental Design, University of California, Berkeley.
REC	*San Francisco Real Estate Circular*
SFD	San Francisco City Directories
SFHA	San Francisco History Archives, Main Library, San Francisco
SFNL	*San Francisco Newsletter*
Tap	Spring Valley Water Company tap records

Location of unique or scarce records are given in parentheses at the end of a listing.

Published Books and Articles:

"Around Russian Hill." *Examiner* Nov. 24, 1889, p. 8, col. 2.

Bancroft's Tourist Guide. San Francisco: A. L. Bancroft and Co., 1871.

"Beautifying Our City," as by "Excelsior." *Bulletin* March 2, 1876, p. 2, col. 3.

Branch, Edgar Marquess, et. al., ed. *Mark Twain's Letters*, Vol. 1, 1853-1866. Berkeley: University of California Press, 1987.

Burgess, Gelett. *The Purple Cow and Other Nonsense.* New York: Dover Books, 1961.

_____. *The Purple Cow and Other Poems.* San Marino, CA: The Huntington Library, 1968.

Burgess, Gelett, Bruce Porter, et. al. *The Lark.* Twenty-four issues (plus an Epi-Lark). Collected in two volumes. San Francisco: William Doxey, 1895-1897.

Coleman, Charles M. *P. G. and E. of California.* New York: McGraw-Hill, 1952.

Collyer, Mabel H. "Russian, the Hill of Those Who Love It." *Call,* Sunday, Dec. , 1912.

Cornelius, Brother. *Keith, Old Master of California.* New York: G. P. Putnam's Sons, 1942.

Cornwall, Bruce. *Life Sketch of Pierre Barlow Cornwall.* San Francisco: A. M. Robertson, 1906.

Dawson, Emma Frances. "A Gracious Visitation," in *An Itinerant House and Other Stories.* San Francisco: William Doxey, 1897.

Dillon, Richard. *Iron Men.* Point Richmond, CA.: Candella Press, 1984.

Freudenheim, Leslie Mandelson, and Elisabeth Sussman. *Building With Nature.* Santa Barbara: Peregrine Smith, Inc., 1974.

Garnett, Porter, ed. *Papers of the San Francisco Vigilance Committee of 1851.* Berkeley: University of California, 1910.

Genthe, Arnold. *As I Remember.* New York: Reynal and Hitchcock, 1936.

Hammond, George P., ed. *The Larkin Papers.* Berkeley: University of California Press, 1963.

Harvey, Genevieve, ed. "Diary of a Trip from Ione to Nevada in 1859," by Susan Mitchell Hall. CHSQ 17 (March, 1938).

Haskins, C. W. *The Argonauts of California.* New York: Fords, Howard and Hulbert., 1890.

"House on a Cliff: The Residence of Mr. Livingston Jenks," *Architectural Record* 20 (Dec. 1906) 489-502.

Hughes, Eden Milton. *Artists in California, 1786-1940.* San Francisco: Hughes Publishing Co., 1986.

Longstreth, Richard. *On the Edge of the World.* New York and Cambridge, Mass.: Architectural History Foundation and MIT Press, 1983. The sources cited in this work pointed the way to much of my research on Willis Polk.

Lord, Eliot. *Comstock Mining and Miners.* Berkeley: Howell-North, 1959 (reprint of 1881 edition).

Lyman, George. *The Saga of the Comstock Lode.* New York: Ballantine Books, 1971 (reprint of the 1934 edition by Charles Scribner's Sons).

Mackay, Margaret. *The Violent Friend.* New York: Doubleday, 1968.

McQuade, Edward. "Neighborhood Characters — Dad Demerest." *San Francisco News,* April 12, 1932.

Meyer, George Homer, et. al. *Municipal Blue Book of San Francisco.* 1915.

Mizner, Addison. *The Many Mizners.* New York, n. d.

Moskowitz, Sam. *History of the Movement.* West Kingston, R. I.: Donald M. Grant, 1980.

_____. "The Science Fiction Hoaxes of William Henry Rhodes," in W. H. Rhodes, *Caxton's Book.* Westport, Conn.: Hyperion Press, 1974.

Motheral, J. G. *Fort Point.* [San Francisco]: Fort Point Museum Association, 1971.

Muhlberger, Richard C. "William H. Ranlett, 19th-Century Architect and Publisher." *Historic Preservation* 22 (Jan.-March 1970) 10-15.

Murdock, Charles. *A Backward Glance at Eighty.* San Francisco: Paul Elder and Co., 1921.

Nathan, Marvin. "San Francisco's *Fin de Siècle* Bohemian Renaissance. CHSQ 61 (Fall 1982) 196-209.

Neider, Charles, ed. *The Selected Letters of Mark Twain.* New York: Harper and Row, 1982.

O'Day, Edward. "Varied Types — Willis Polk." *Town Talk* (Feb. 25, 1911)

Paul, Almarin Brooks. "My First Two Years in California." *Quarterly of the Society of California Pioneers* 4 (March 31, 1927) 24-54.

Peixotto, Ernest. "Architecture in San Francisco." *Overland Monthly* (May, 1893) 449-463.

Polk, Willis. *A Matter of Taste,* ed. by Richard Longstreth. San Francisco: Book Club of California. 1979.

_____. *Architectural News.* Three issues, 1890-1891. (DOCS)

Ranlett, William H. *The Architect.* New York: W. H. Graham, 1847. Republished by Dewitt and Davenport, New York, 1849-1851. (In 1976 Da Capo Press, New York, published a reprint of the latter edition.)

Rassmussen, Louis J. *San Francisco Ship Passenger Lists,* Vol. 2. Colma, CA: San Francisco Historic Records, 1966.

Rhodes, William H. *Caxton's Book,* ed. by Daniel O'Connell. San Francisco: Bancroft and Co., 1876. (Reprinted by Hyperion Press, Westport, Conn., in 1974.)

Roos, Robert. "Houses Out of San Francisco History." San Francisco News, Nov. 5, 1941.

Scully, Vincent. *The Shingle Style and the Stick Style.* New Haven, Conn.: Yale University Press, 1971.

Shuck, Oscar T. *History of the Bench and Bar of California.* Los Angeles, 1901.

Smith, Grant H. *The History of the Comstock Lode, 1850-1920.* Reno: Nevada State Bureau of Mines, 7th printing (revised), 1970.

Soule, Frank, John H. Gihon, and James Nisbett. *The Annals of San Francisco.* New York: D. Appleton and Co., 1855.

Steffens, Lincoln. *Autobiography.* New York: Harcourt, Brace and Co., 1931.

Sullivan, G. W. *Early Days in California.* Enterprise Publishing Co., 1888.

Swasey, W. F. *The Early Days and men of California.* Oakland: Pacific Press Publishing Co., 1891.

Thompson, Elisabeth Kendall. "The Early Domestic Architecture of the San Francisco Bay Region." *Journal of the Society of Architectural Historians* 10 (Oct. 1951) 18.

Walker, Franklin. *San Francisco's Literary Frontier.* New York: Alfred A. Knopf, 1939.

Wheat, Carl I., ed. "California's Bantam Cock," CHSQ 10 (Sept. 1931).

Wilder, Laura Ingalls. *West from Home*, ed. by Roger Lea MacBride. New York: Harper and Row, 1974.

Letters, Manuscripts, Typescripts, Dissertation, Papers, and Pamphlets:

"A Brief Account of the Institution of the San Francisco Society of the New Jerusalem." San Francisco: 1870. (Swedenborgian Church)

Atkinson, Kate. *The Home.* Privately printed, 1910. (Bancroft)

Backus, Joseph Moorhead. "Gelett Burgess: A Biography of the Man Who Wrote the Purple Cow." PhD. diss., University of California, n.d. [ca. early 1960s]. This work was essential to my understanding of Burgess' personality and career.

Burgess, Frank Gelett. Diaries, 1891-1891. Burgess Papers. (Bancroft)

California Art Research, Vol. 5. San Francisco: Works Progress Administration, 1937. (SFHA)

Cabot, Richard C. Letter to Mrs. Arthur (Susie) Lyman, 1901. (Swedenborgian Church)

Demerest, Frank. Demerest file. (SFHA)

Dinnean, Lawrence. "Les Jeunes," ed. by J. R. K. Kantor. Friends of the Bancroft Library, 1980. Issued to accompany a Bancroft Library exhibition.

Drury, Aubrey. *The Livermore Family.* (Bancroft Library)

Gillespie and Gray, Attorneys. "Information from an Abstract of Title and Certificate of Search of Lot 810." San Francisco: 1860. This is a title search by Gillespie and Gray of the Ranlett residence from 1848-1860, with updates to 1895. (Author's possession)

Gray, Cyril V. "Appellant's Brief: In the Supreme Court of the State of California, George D. Nagle vs. Charles Homer." San Francisco: Charles A. Calhoun, printer, 1857. (Bancroft)

Gray, Nathaniel. Biographical material, folder 5. (Bancroft)

Homer, Charles. Cash Book and Ledger, 1851-1854. (Bancroft)

_____. Charles Homer Letters. (CHS)

Kast, Agnes. "Declaration of Agnes Kast." October 23, 1977. (Author's possession)

Keeler, Charles. *Friends Bearing Torches.* (Bancroft)

Lawrence, James F. "Working Draft of an Essay on Joseph Worcester." 1993.

Livermore, George. "One Hundred Years of Livermore on Russian Hill." In Gardner W. Mein's real estate newsletter, 1990.

Lone Mountain Cemetery Records. (Society of California Pioneers)

Maybeck, Bernard. Letter to Willis Polk, March 6, 1915. (Polk Papers, DOCS)

Martinez, Elsie Whitaker. *Elsie Whitaker Martinez.* Interview by the Regional Oral History Office, Bancroft Library, 1969. (Bancroft)

Morphy, Edward. *San Francisco's Thoroughfares.* First published as a column in the *Chronicle,* 1919-1920. Collected as a typescript (SFHA) and in the "S. F. Streets" scrapbook (CHS).

Muhlberger, Richard C. Unpublished monograph on William H. Ranlett.

Paul, Almarin Brooks. "Biographical Sketch of the Life of Almarin B. Paul, written by Himself." Manuscript, written 1879-1883. (CHS)

Pioneer Scrapbooks. (Society of California Pioneers)

Polk, Willis. Letter to Irving M. Scott, Oct. 26, 1894. Polk Papers. (DOCS)

_____. Polk Papers. (DOCS)

Porter, Bruce. Letter to Willis Polk, May 21, 1917. (Polk Papers, DOCS)

Records from Tombstones in Laurel Hill Cemetery, 1853-1937. (SFHA)

San Francisco Cemetery Records, 1848-1863. 1938. (SFHA)

Sears, Edmund H. "Joseph Worcester." 1930. (Swedenborgian Church)

Spencer, Eldrege T. Plan of 1030 Vallejo. 1945. (DOCS)

Unitarian Church membership and pew rental records. (Unitarian Church)

Wheeler, Alfred. *Land Titles in San Francisco, and the Laws Affecting the Same.* N. p., 1852. (SFHA)

Worcester, Alfred. Letter to Edmund H. Sears, 1930. (Swedenborgian Church)

_____. "Rev. Joseph Worcester, A Memoir and Extracts from his Letters to his Nephew, Alfred Worcester." 1945. (Swedenborgian Church)

Worcester, Joseph. Joseph Worcester Collection. This was Worcester's library of architectural books and periodicals. (DOCS)

Interviews by the Author

Roger Jobson. Oct. 15, 1987.

George Livermore. March 30 and April 7, 1988.

Jaques Schnier. March 28, 1984 and March 8, 1985.

City Property Records, etc.

Despite the loss of many city records in the fire of 1906, enough survive to enable one to create a chain of title for most properties in San Francisco. The use of these records enabled me to research the origins of many houses, and to understand Charles Homer's central role as the founder of the Summit neighborhood.

City records used included:

General Index. This is an index to all real estate transactions in San Francisco, and survives complete from the late 1840s to 1906. (SFHA)

Index to Deeds. This is an index to deed transactions only. Surviving volumes cover the late 1840s through 1853, and 1885-1906. (SFHA)

Deeds. These are verbatim copies of property deeds. Surviving volumes include all volumes through early 1854, scattered volumes in the 1860s, and a complete run from 1894 to 1906. (SFHA)

McEnerney Judgments ("Quiet Title"). Because of the loss of many city records in 1906, owners of property in San Francisco had to file claims with the city and show proof of ownership. These records can be found on microfilm at the County Clerk's Office.

Other records pertaining to buildings and property include:

Spring Valley Water Co. Tap Records. This is a compilation of the Application for Service Installation (ASI) records of the Spring Valley company. Records began in 1861. They later became part of the city's water department records, and can now be found on microfilm at the SFHA.

San Francisco Real Estate Circular. From 1868-1887 this periodical noted the sale of property in San Francisco. (SFHA)

San Francisco Newsletter. From 1865-1887 this periodical printed abstracts of deeds. (Sutro Library)

Sanborn Insurance Maps. These maps show the footprints of all buildings in the densely developed areas of the city. For the Summit, available years include 1885, 1891, 1899, 1905, 1912, 1913. All of these can be found on microfilm at the SFHA.

Coast Survey Maps. These maps show contours of the land and the extent of development in the city for 1852, 1857, 1869, and ca. 1881. The 1857 map (published in 1859) is especially accurate in showing individual buildings.

Butler's Map of the City of San Francisco. 1854. This map shows individual buildings with a high degree of accuracy. (SFHA)

INDEX

(Residences on Russian Hill are listed at the end. Page numbers after 115 refer to notes.)

Index to Russian Hill Residences